Wealth Inside Out

Wealth Inside Out expertly guides you on how to pinpoint what truly matters in your life, and more importantly, how to have the courage to step into it. —Raymond Aaron, coauthor, *Chicken Soup for The Parents Soul*

If you are not satisfied with the way your life has turned out and aren't sure what to do about it, *Wealth Inside Out* is a good place to start. Mark and Desirée present the steps from discontent with your lot in the world (even amid your success) to living your passion and dreams. —Morty Lefkoe, cofounder of the Lefkoe Institute, author *Re-create Your Life*

Reading this book was a gift to my life and purpose. I loved Mark's conversations with the Wizard and took many notes on the inspired messages. —Margaret Merrill, author *Live the Life You Love*

Wealth Inside Out especially succeeds because it *interprets* and makes Mark's personal experience accessible to others. The big "take away" is a highly intuitive and usable framework for achieving true wealth and happiness. —Barry Heermann, author of *Noble Purpose, Igniting Extraordinary Passion in Life and Work*

Obtain Your

Wealth Creation Workbook **Here**

The easiest way gain the most benefit from this book, is to take advantage of our special offering. The *Wealth Creation Workbook* will help you generate fresh insights and new understanding about your most cherished aspirations and how to create true wealth. You will more easily integrate what you learn through reading *Wealth Inside Out*.

Through a series of compelling questions, the *Wealth Creation Workbook* will lead you step-by-step through each of the Six Dimensions of Wealth Creation to a clear focused vision for your life and how you will achieve wealth from the inside out.

You can download your workbook immediately

for only $11.97

(Regularly $37, You Save $25.03)

Download Your Special
***Wealth Creation Workbook* Today at**
www.WealthCreationWorkbook.com

Enter Promotional Code: True Wealth

Wealth Inside Out

How I Found True Wealth

in Work, Life and Play and

How You Can Too

By Mark Watson
Reflections by Desirée Watson

Published byBascom Hill Publishing Group

Mark Watson
Wealth Inside Out: How I Found True Wealth in Work, Life and Play and How You Can Too: / Mark Watson

ISBN: 978-0-9798467-1-7
ISBN: 0-9798467-1-4
LCCN: 2008921739
Success / Business / Motivation / Money Psychology / Personal Growth

Printed in the United States of America

This material has been written solely for educational purposes. Some or all of the strategies and ideas outlined in this book may not be suitable for your situation. All business and investment activities have inherent risks, and no information presented by or through this book should be taken as a recommendation to make specific entrepreneurial or investment decisions without consulting your own legal, tax, accounting, investment, financial planning, business or other professional. Further, the authors specifically encourage you to seek such independent, competent advice before making any entrepreneurial or investment decision.

Neither do the authors dispense medical advice or prescribe the use of any technique as a form of treatment for physical, emotional or medical problems without the advice of a licensed medical professional, either directly or indirectly.

The intent of the authors is to offer information only of a general nature to assist in your quest for greater success and happiness. In the event you use any of the information in this book for yourself, the Authors and Publisher(s) assume no responsibility for your actions. The Author and Publisher specifically disclaim any liability, loss, damage or risk which is incurred or alleged to be incurred as a consequence, directly or indirectly, of the use and application of any of the contents of this work.

Although the stories in this book are true, the characters and events are intended to be enjoyed and to teach rather than to be a precise factual recount.

Contents

The Purpose of This Book

Wealth Inside Out is dedicated to people who want to achieve true wealth and happiness in their personal and professional lives. This happens more easily when you are connected accurately with what matters to you. When you have a clear sense of purpose and direction plus a roadmap to get there, the true wealth opportunities begin to open up and your life takes on a new momentum.

My intention and the goal of the book are to make it easier for you to create greater wealth and happiness in all areas of your life—financially, interpersonally, physically and spiritually—and to be perpetually in touch with your interior source of clarity and confidence. This extraordinary *inner* technology gives you improved mental aptitude for achieving the success and happiness that results when you do what you love and follow your dreams.

Those who may find *Wealth Inside Out* particularly useful:

- People Who Are at a Crossroads in Their Business or Personal Life

- People Who Want to Do What They Love and Make Money

- Successful People Who Feel Like Something Is Missing

- People in Transition Who Want to Find Clear Direction

- Anyone Who Has Ever Purchased a Product or Seminar Training about How to Make Money Including Programs on Stock Trading, Real Estate Investing, Internet Marketing, or Starting a Business

- People Feeling Stuck Who Want to Learn How to Become Successful

- Entrepreneurs, Investors and Business Owners Who Want to Avoid the Most Costly Wealth Creation Mistakes

- Coaches, Consultants and Healing Professionals Who Want Powerful New Tools to Help Their Clients Achieve Greater Success and Happiness

- People Who Want to Learn How to Harness the Power of Their Passions and Turn Them into Wealth

- Anyone Who Is Ready for True Success and Happiness in Any Area of Life

Foreword

In the book you are holding in your hands, Mark Watson shares a truly remarkable story. After much hard work, Mark and his wife Desirée had achieved a high level of financial success. However, Mark found his life was lacking the sense of purpose and deeper meaning which he thought would automatically come with more money. As often happens with many other people who achieve financial success, Mark found that the higher and more complete levels of fulfillment and contentment still eluded him.

Growing and managing a large construction company, a sizeable apartment complex and managing a stock and mutual fund portfolio became a major struggle in the face of Mark's discontent. The toll this struggle took was so great that Mark Watson (an otherwise strong and healthy man) thought he was having a heart attack.

No doctor was able to help him identify the cause of his heart palpitations. His anguish became the source of his strength and power that provided the impetus and motivation for Mark to crystallize and condense his 20-plus years of insights from studying human achievement.

The end result was a remarkably powerful and easy-to-use set of tools, techniques, exercises and strategies that Mark and Desirée Watson are now sharing with their students and clients in trainings, retreats, coaching and mentoring programs all across the United States and Canada.

In reading *Wealth Inside Out* you'll have a front row seat to witness firsthand the excitement and drama that Mark experienced on this extraordinary journey. And most importantly, you'll learn how to use some of the powerful strategies and exercises that Mark and Desirée developed to help their clients achieve their most important wealth goals.

As a veteran psychologist and business mentor, I have had the opportunity to speak and work with more than 10,000 students and clients over the last 25 years including some of the world's top seminar speakers, investors and business executives. It is noteworthy that Mark

Watson has the ability to develop such powerful wealth development processes and to share these breakthrough techniques with others. Also impressive are Mark and Desirée's sincerity and their dedication to helping others achieve wealth in all aspects of their lives.

Mark and Desirée Watson's trainings are enriching, empowering and transformative.

Sincerely,
Donald Moine, PhD
Business Psychologist
Palos Verdes, California
www.drmoine.com

Introduction

By Barry Heermann

Mark asked me to write this introduction long ago when he first began scripting his book. This was not because I was famous or didn't know the author, as is customary in the world of books, but for exactly the opposite reason. I knew Mark fairly well, and my life has shifted as a result of what I witnessed through his extraordinary personal journey.

Mark today is unrecognizable compared with the Mark whom I first met. I have never known anyone to shift his life so radically. Mark surrendered full-heartedly to his essential self—to the still voice within. He actually found comfort and solace in not knowing where he was headed. He gave up control, asked for guidance and received it. He accessed vast equanimity and discovered his own inner joy. And through his surrender and release, he wrote this inspiring book that recounts every step of the way.

What distinguishes this book from virtually every other book on the subjects of wealth creation and finding your purpose in life is that it arises out of the author's authentic experience of "hitting the wall" and the transformation that resulted. The book stands on the merits of this remarkable story alone. But *Wealth Inside Out* especially succeeds because it *interprets* and makes this experience accessible to others... without one having to first strike the wall. The big "take away" is a highly intuitive and usable framework for effortlessly achieving true success and happiness.

My encounter with Mark Watson began in January, 2004, when my wife and I moved from San Diego to Carmel by the Sea. Good friend Theo Cade, who valued Mark both as successful contractor and creator of personal development programs, had recommended we get in touch with him. He helped us acquire our home and get oriented when we first arrived.

Shortly thereafter, we began to meet with Mark and his wife Desirée, as well as their good friends Annee and David. Then "R-Group" (short for "Our Group") was born as we agreed to have dinner and share some evenings together, with each couple facilitating a discussion during our biweekly, rotating sessions.

During one R-Group session, Mark announced that he was recommitting himself to his career as a contractor, even though this was no longer fulfilling. To reach a certain financial goal, he would buckle under and tough it out so that he and Desirée could be financially free. He sought out a rigorous coach, a real taskmaster who offered a program that would help him take control and achieve his goal, he hoped in five years.

During our meetings, Mark would report on his journey, his intention and his frustration. No, it was not what he loved to do, but yes, he would drive to accomplish what he wanted. He rigidly stayed the course. Yet, to me he seemed completely removed and unclear. I was concerned that such a resolute strategy would backfire on him in some way.

I found it painful watching Mark go through this, yet he did not seem ready to hear other perspectives on the matter. Really, I was drawn to the Mark that I glimpsed below the surface—the innocent, relaxed and loving man who had so much zest for life. I found myself powerfully moved by the Mark who would play his guitar while singing beautifully, rapturously. Yet, over the weeks and months that followed, I began to feel inauthentic and reserved as I pulled away from Mark.

Then one day while sitting in a Carmel eatery, Mark and I had a rather lively conversation as we both expressed what had been withheld. Sitting in Mark's car after lunch, we had a meeting of the minds, a meeting of our hearts…and a clearing of the air. We expressed our appreciation for the friendship we shared, and we made requests of each other. Mark wanted to be heard without me making him wrong. I wanted to be acknowledged for my support and contribution to him. We reached an accord of sorts.

It seems that Mark's journey afforded him a kind of cracking open, and with it an awakening. A new reality emerged. That process of cracking open and how he responded is the story Mark tells so eloquently in this book. It is an adventure, but more than this it is a story of remarkable personal transformation that others can use to find their way toward true wealth and happiness.

I am honored to enjoy Mark's friendship. Today, a mysterious kind of living water washes over him and his life. You cannot read this book and avoid—one minute longer—being removed from that which is most essential within you. Mark demonstrates how to engage the inner divine, on purpose. Take him seriously, as I have learned to do.

You have heard the old adage: Behind every success story is a caring and committed partner. During the personal transitions that both Desiree and Mark encountered, Desirée was truly the grounding force, the guiding light and the strongest proponent of following the path upon which they both felt compelled to follow. Although the story is told through Mark's frame of reference, you might say Desirée is the "spiritual director" in their partnership. She is the one who most encouraged the new openings in perspective and kept Mark focused upon finding the highest wisdom within his heart. Desirée's own surrender is inextricably linked to the changes Mark encountered and the resulting discovery of *Wealth Inside Out* for both of them. That is part of the greatness of this book. The gifts you will find within these pages are really an immense contribution to the world from both Mark and Desirée.

Barry Heermann, March, 2008, author *Noble
Purpose, Igniting Extraordinary Passion in Life and Work*

*The greatest good you can do for another is not just
to share your riches, but to reveal to him [or her] his own.*
Benjamin Disraeli, former British Prime Minister (1804-1881)

Preface

Every noble work is at first impossible.
—Thomas Carlyle, Scottish philosopher (1795-1881)

One of the secrets of true wealth creation is to do what you love. When you discover *how* to do what you love, success comes naturally, and you will more easily achieve the happiness you desire.

Wealth Inside Out offers a practical, easy-to-follow roadmap that will turbocharge your ability find the work of your heart so that true wealth can be yours too. You will discover how to follow your dreams and do what you have always wanted. You'll learn how to achieve financial, interpersonal, physical and spiritual wealth. The journey is one of discovering your true nature, and it will guide you to a life of happiness and contentment.

Before we begin, I'd like to say a few words about the methodology of the book. The processes outlined within these pages are designed to open up clear passage to what is naturally seeking expression from within you, yet *Wealth Inside Out* is not meant to be a formulaic essay. Your own journey to finding true wealth will be *your* unique discovery. And the processes outlined in this book will powerfully help you find your way, as long as you are willing to engage these principles and apply them in your life. The primary questions you will answer from reading this book are, What is fully possible for your life and how can you begin to do what you love right now? Once you take this to heart and indeed apply the principles of *Wealth Inside Out*, I may even include your success story in my next book. I invite you to send them to me.

One of the powerful principles that you will learn about is that ordinary logic and traditional wisdom—what is often considered to be the "proven"—can at times be the very obstacle that gets in your way of finding true success and happiness. It was for me, and surely has been for many others throughout time.

To illustrate my point, consider that the visionaries of humankind (inventors, authors and entrepreneurs alike) are the ones leading the way. This is true not because they are famous or write perfectly or follow what has already been done, but in following their dreams and doing what they love, they capture something beyond the ordinary. It may be an inspirational concept, a unique energy or a perspective that rings true for a particular time. Really, what we know to be factual is no more than a snapshot of what we understand about a particular subject at any given point.

For example, I grew up near the home of Thomas Jefferson and visited his mansion known as Monticello many times. Located in one of the rooms is a duplicating device. It consists of a few wooden sticks hinged in such a way that by writing with one pen, a second pen will copy what one is writing onto another piece of paper. Do you think that Thomas Jefferson could have predicted the computer science or the aerospace technology of today?

Certainly, one should not ignore the wisdom and knowledge gained through traditional protocols of science and human achievement. However, beyond the cultural spell of following what you already know is the quiet inner confidence imbedded deep within you. That is where *your* unique path to wealth creation will begin to emerge and take form. So the question is not so much about what I have captured through writing this book; you want to focus on What is the extraordinary passion for life that you are here to capture? How can you do what you love and embrace *your* natural way of creating wealth and finding happiness? Will you take the steps to finally do what you love and create wealth from the inside out? *Wealth Inside Out* will show you how to begin.

Chapter One

FIND YOUR COMPASS

Navigating Life with Guidance and A True Wealth Vision

We must be willing to get rid of the life we've planned,
so as to have the life that is waiting for us.
—Joseph Campbell, American writer (1904-1987)

I've always been fascinated by people who seem passionate about what they are doing. Often I have wondered how it is that some people get to do what they really want and others never seem to. What are the dynamics that allow some people to create financial wealth, satisfying relationships, physical vitality, and a deep inner peace with life? *Wealth Inside Out* is about creating wealth in every area of your life, which includes financial, interpersonal, physical and spiritual wealth.

The journey to Wealth Inside Out begins with *your* passions. Wealth and happiness follow naturally. Have you ever noticed that those who are passionate have identified a vision that, almost automatically, keeps them on course with a sense of meaning and purpose? This kind of vision is not usually a made-up idea—it comes from deep within, like a sparkle of life from beyond one's DNA.

The good news is that anyone who is willing to follow a few basic principles can have this passion for life, too. First, you must discover your purpose and the true wealth vision inside of you. You need clear direction to land successfully on your ideal wealth-building niche—one that will work just right for you and make you successful. You need to learn how to navigate your way to wealth creation in each area of your life. *Wealth Inside Out* will give you the confidence. You will also need powerful tools and skills to move past the limitations of your mind, which you will learn more about as we go along. Finally, you will need the help of expert mentors who will show you how to harness the power of your passions and turn them into wealth.

When you open yourself to fresh understanding and apply several dynamics, a new personal power is unleashed. From there you are able to reorganize your focus and pursue the deepest callings of your heart.

My journey to Wealth Inside Out began with an unexpected bolt from the blue. One morning while working at the computer, I began to feel dizzy. My heart was racing, and I had a sense of panic. Calling for my wife Desirée, I gasped, "Honey, you better take me to the emergency room. I think I'm having a heart attack."

I made it into the living room and fell on my knees while holding the back of the sofa. Nearly breathless, I wondered if this was it. Could my life possibly end this way, without ever expressing the dreams I had held inside? My real life's work had not even begun, and my purpose was unfulfilled. What I did not yet understand was that my symptoms indeed marked the beginning of the new life that was waiting for me.

Everyone wants a good life, absolutely everyone. Regardless of income or sociocultural background, we want the same thing—to live happily and to be successful. We want satisfying work, connected relationships, financial freedom, physical vitality and a life that matters.

There is also a special dream in each of us that wants to happen. We want to know our purpose in life, fulfill our passions and do what we love. This is what I call Wealth Inside Out. The more common references to wealth are

> To know your purpose is to understand where you belong in life. It's about why you are here and what you were born to do.

in terms of only money and material riches, yet true wealth—Wealth Inside Out—is about the quality of your whole life. Wealth simply means "well being," which includes all aspects of your life. True wealth comes to you once you discover and activate your life purpose. Some people seem to find this easily; others work hard at it. Many spend their entire existence looking, and even more give up altogether.

There is no need to give up. Finding your purpose in life happens naturally by activating the passions inside of you. This is the first step toward true success and happiness. Now you need a way to get there. You have to find your compass. Much like a bird flies south for the winter and a whale navigates thousands of miles every year, you have an internal navigation system for finding true happiness and clear direction. All it takes to get on your path is a willingness to become skilled at a few simple practices that you'll learn about in this book.

To know your purpose is to understand where you belong in life. It's about why you are here and what you were born to do. It is about fulfilling the desires of your heart and soul. Without purpose, you can feel lost and never quite sure how to direct your attention. When you are clear, however, the things that matter come together more easily and you begin to experience true wealth and happiness. Knowing your purpose acts as your anchor, rudder and sail. Life automatically becomes better.

This book is borne out of personal experience—an unexpected quest to follow my inner rumblings. Although I had explored ways of finding true wealth and getting my life on track, none of them quite worked until I stumbled upon the internal guiding process that would lead me there. I found my compass. Now my purpose includes helping you find yours.

When I first started writing, I was stymied, and I mean completely blocked. I was yearning to find my niche and become aligned with it. I was looking for a joyful way to earn my living and create wealth, yet ordinary logic had me imagining the future through the same lens that was keeping me stuck. The more I tried to figure it out, the less clear I became. I had all but given up.

I'll admit I was feeling insecure and frightened, and yet my intuitive whispers still brought twinges of excitement and freedom. It was time to go after my higher purpose—that predominant human call to find what I was born to do. Life was calling me to enter a new dimension of understanding beyond what I had previously known. Compelled to follow this primary guiding force, I adopted it as my compass.

Buckle Your Seat Belt

One morning while we were discussing opportunities for the future, Desirée said, "Honey, buckle your seat belt; we're going on a God ride." This was her way of saying big changes were brewing. We looked at each other knowing that what was unfolding was bigger than anything we had ever encountered. Our strategic approach to success was no longer taking us where we wanted to go. Now something unavoidable was happening in spite of our doubts and fears; the biggest challenge would be to get out of the way.

For a long time, I was not in touch with a higher purpose. I had no compass. Upon first putting pen to paper, I had no idea that a book was being written. I simply began to keep a journal of the inner whispers I was hearing. Initially, I found the whispers unnerving, but I was even more afraid to ignore them. This left me no choice other than to surrender to the unseen machinery of life.

Later, I realized I was beginning to write a book about wealth and finding your purpose in life. But how was I to do this when I was still looking for my own? This was illogical to my ordinary way of thinking, a bit of a Catch-22.

Nevertheless, a different way of living emerged for me, as it can for you. Although you'll read stories about my personal journey, the book is intended to inspire you to find your passion and follow your dreams. What is that special thing that you feel *called* to do?

Notice how you feel inside as you read these words. Are you excited? Fearful? Skeptical? Perhaps all of these are true. I know they were for me. What I find fascinating is that through composing this book, my purpose in life became clear.

Writing *Wealth Inside Out* taught me that things don't always work the way I think they should. I was locked into a belief that life operates only in a logical, step-by-step manner. Following these steps would surely take me where I wanted to go. Was I ever surprised to learn about an easier, more natural way of being. It is this "new" way that provides the foundation for what you are about to read. So buckle your seat belt for a ride into the heart of your dreams.

The Secret Power

For a long time, I did not know that my deepest desire is always to feel connected with the natural laws of creation and my unique contribution to life. Neither did I understand that it could be as effortless as breathing to hear and understand what had been previously unknown. It took a shift in perception before I could communicate with this fundamental knowing and follow a new path toward true success and happiness—a path that felt expansive and freeing.

I began to ponder the question: What is the most powerful organizing principle in the universe? Scientists call it Energy or the Quantum Field of Creation. Religions often refer to it as a supreme deity, although many would not link the name of God solely with the forces studied by science. Others simply call it Nature or say they just don't know, and atheists say it may not exist, at least not by the name of God. Psychologists term it the Higher Self and Subconscious Mind and other traditions call it the Self or Flow of Life. Native peoples call it Great Spirit. I've also heard this prime cause called Universal Spirit, Divine Intelligence, Higher Power and so on.

What matters is not the name but the *relationship* we have with the very source of creation. I am not talking about some obscure notion, but a reliable inner well of communion where we find clear direction and connect with our purpose in life. This relationship is the secret power of the universe. It is the cornerstone of tremendous strength and power, and you can use this power to create true wealth in every area of your life. While not understood completely, it is accessible to anyone who is willing to make the call.

As a fellow human, I am a spiritual being, linked to the infinite universe that embraces us all. I believe that every person is a unique expression of this unlimited power and that neither you nor I would be here without it.

Wizard

Mix a little foolishness with your serious plans.
It is lovely to be silly at the right moment.
—Horace, Greek poet (65BC-8BC)

My own relationship with the secret power developed by fits and starts. I had my share of counter beliefs and socialized misapprehension, mostly based in ordinary logic.

But I was also blessed with profound inner earthquakes. Eventually, I began to realize that a part of us simply *knows*. Something in us transcends ordinary logic and conscious understanding, putting us in a beneficial relationship with life. We can ask any question, and answers appear if we are willing to listen. For me, it was as if I had an intelligent wizard inside who *wanted* to direct me to my purpose and to Wealth Inside Out. Moreover, this wise inner messenger had no limitations concerning thought, time, energy and resources. The *Wizard* therefore brought me more in touch with nature's infinite power. His messages came as guidance from within my heart, the place that simply knows. Clearly, the guidance was leading me on a journey that felt most expansive—a path still taking me to what I believe is my highest purpose.

As you read these pages, please don't get stuck on the language I use. I've had to endure near ridicule for crafting such characterizations of the voices inside my mind, but what the heck? They make my point, and most people begin to have the same kind of fun with their own inner voices. Whether your beliefs are like mine or otherwise, the principles I outline are for everyone and make possible a life of true success and happiness. Use your own language if it helps you grasp the primary message. That is, you can access the clarity of *your* innermost wisdom to find your purpose in life, create true wealth and get your life on track. The internal navigation technology discussed throughout this book connects you with your passion for life and the dreams inside your soul. This wonderful secret power is really meant for us all.

Sneaky Pete

The Wizard's opponent, Sneaky Pete, is a character I imagine to represent the shadowed side of my psyche. Sneaky Pete embodies the negative beliefs of limitation and my unconscious programming. He is an alter ego, the critical voice inside my head who acts as prosecutor, judge and jury. He says things such as, "You can't do what you really want," or "You're not good enough, smart enough, educated enough..." and the like.

But Sneaky Pete has a narrow view of reality and is always sure that his erroneous views are correct. Hiding out in the crevices of my subconscious, he emerges just in time to try to kill my dreams. He concocts devious schemes as he looks for opportunities to sabotage my goals. Why do you think his first name is Sneaky?

Though Sneaky Pete is a character that supposedly I made up, his influence on me was very real as I was finding my way to Wealth Inside Out. He worked hard to rattle my confidence. Though he always tried to stop me, I gained momentum toward my dreams when I learned to face his undermining ways head on. This is something you will learn how to do as well.

Five Forces

In all, I have identified five primary forces that work in synergy:

1. You can begin with the Wizard and the voice of possibility. This will keep you in touch with infinite creation and the fundamental organizing principles of life.

2. Guidance comes naturally as intuitive whispers from your inner source of higher wisdom. You'll also need the guidance of experts who will help you learn how to become successful and create wealth.

3. Watch out for Sneaky Pete and your limiting beliefs. Don't let your inner critic and saboteur get in the way of your dreams.

4. Your purpose in life reflects what you feel compelled to express in the world. How can you do what you love, follow your dreams and shape your life around what you most value?

5. Your personal reactions and reflections about each experience will help you integrate what you must know. Learn to take pleasure in both your inner and outer journey.

Wealth Inside Out tells a story about how I learned to interact with these sometimes complex and polarized influences, finding my place of equilibrium amid a mix of inner voices. For example, I began to distinguish momentary personal preferences from my core passionate stirrings. I also came to terms with our common plight as humans, finding happiness and more satisfying ways to be alive.

For one thing, I had feelings of fulfillment not necessarily related to any material accomplishment. I was more confident, patient and realistic about everyday matters. Life became less of a struggle and more of an adventure. In addition, I started to enjoy waking up each day to the aliveness of my heart's desire. Each time I followed my Wizard instead of Sneaky Pete, I was rewarded with more courage and clarity.

Everybody has a purpose in life and an inner voice of higher wisdom. Everybody has a Sneaky Pete. And our responses to the voices inside ourselves have much to do with how we create wealth and our quality of life. Which voice will you listen to?

Finding Purpose

Your work is to discover your
work and then give yourself to it.
—The Buddha (563 BC-483 BC)

Finding purpose is about asking for clarity from the infinite, and recognizing your inner source of knowing. Finding your mission in life involves tuning in to the deepest parts of your being, then having the

> All of us know on some level what our higher purpose is, but many of us have disconnected with it.

willingness to follow the inner guidance you receive. Using this powerful process you will discover the way to true wealth creation in every area of your life. You will uncover useful solutions and identify resources for any problem or challenge you face. You will get answers about your life direction, finances, relationships and your physical health. You will also open up a powerful connection with the very source of creation, which will compel you to generate positive outcomes in all aspects of your life.

For some, Wealth Inside Out comes easily; others may get stuck for a while. If you become overly driven in your quest for inner guidance, your mind may drown out those gentle whispers and cause your purpose to elude you. Yet, if you do not focus on finding your purpose in life and living your passions, your inner rumblings and clarity may never get through. When you simply ask for help and allow answers to come, new doors open. Walking through them will change your life—if you are willing to take the first steps.

One thing is certain: When you engage the possibility of a true life purpose, true wealth becomes difficult to avoid. Your rumblings will intensify their purpose to find expression in the world. Once you are clear and step into this powerful influence, your life will never again be the same. That is something I can promise.

*Give to the world the best you have, and
the best will come back to you.*
Ella Wheeler Wilcox, American poet and journalist (1850-1919)

Chapter Two

WHAT'S MY PURPOSE?

Traveling the Six Dimensions of Wealth Creation

A musician must make music, an artist must paint, a poet must write, if he
[or she] is to be ultimately at peace with himself. What a man can be, he must be.
— Abraham Maslow, American psychologist (1908-1970)

There are many benefits to finding your purpose in life. It is the first step toward wealth creation, true success and happiness. When you know your purpose, you feel more connected, make better decisions, you have more fun, and life feels good.

Finding your purpose in life usually begins with an inner, perhaps unexplainable urge—a grand restlessness that seeks expression. Then is the question of taking action (or not) while moving past fear and limitation. To go forward you must begin asking new questions as you learn how to navigate your way to true fulfillment and Wealth Inside Out. Clarity comes once you have the tools and skills for being in sync with your deepest goals and dreams.

I discovered this the hard way. Now you can benefit from my experiences, so you don't have to make the same mistakes.

Seeking Clarity

Desirée and I worked and lived in Carmel, California, and we owned 72 apartment units in Oklahoma. In construction, we did well financially, but I was burned out on building. We enjoyed the apartment business but needed to generate additional cash flow while growing our real estate portfolio. At least that was the plan.

Although we had looked at dozens of other businesses, none held our interest. With our strategy for gaining clarity not clicking into place, we were swimming upstream. Then we took a workshop on finding your purpose in life. Like many others, I had often thought of what I might *like* to do, keeping in mind what seemed logical. I had also contemplated the meaning of life, but not in the context of my particular *purpose.*

I could sense that my purpose revolved around helping others in their achievement of life goals and building their dreams. What wasn't clear was exactly *how* to do this. Desirée and I decided we should first stabilize our financial wealth, which would then free us to pursue our real passions. Both of us liked the world of personal growth, and we often talked about how one day we would work together in that field.

Many people get stuck this way, thinking that *one day* they will get to do what they really want. Others fall in the trap of believing they have to get money handled before they can do what they want. Money plays a part, but most successful people do not start off with money. We didn't. They begin with a dream and then learn how to put the money around that. This is how you create wealth from the inside out.

Take a look in your own life. Are you waiting for money to begin a dream? What is the someday that you are waiting for? What if you could follow your dreams right now without even knowing how to begin?

A few weeks later, Desirée and I began a comprehensive organizational training for business development. We took tests and set goals. After several months of exploration and planning, we still were not clear about what steps to take. We were fast using up our resources and eager to bring in more money. Only later did I realize the extent of my deeper call.

Reluctantly, we postponed our rumblings for the field of personal development and decided to reorganize our construction business to sell it in five years. This is what made the most sense. With our new business knowledge, Desirée and I would establish management systems to grow the company. Logically, I knew this approach could resolve our financial ambitions, and I became excited about putting it together in a new way. We did all the homework, assembled our plan and off we went, or so I thought.

What happened instead was that for the first time in my construction career, I was unable to find work. Desirée and I were meeting with architects and prospective clients, but no one was buying. There was plenty of work in the area, so that wasn't a problem. When I had needed work in the past, I could make a few phone calls, and it appeared like magic. But now it seemed my magic was lost. I wondered what we were going to do.

What Is Calling You?

None of us will ever accomplish anything excellent or commanding except when he [or she] listens to this whisper which is heard by him alone.
— Ralph Waldo Emerson, American essayist and poet (1803-1882)

What I had difficulty grasping was that one's priorities are not necessarily those a person *thinks* are best, but those that speak from the heart. For example, what comes to your mind when I ask the question: What do you *really* want in life? Do your answers bring you greater clarity or more confusion?

I felt expanded by what we had learned from the organizational training, and it was an important catalyst for what would come next. However, I had not yet touched on one essential link. Now I was face-to-face with the incongruity between logic and my deeper desires. It was time to clarify my true wealth priorities. This is something you will want to do as well.

As I considered what to do next, I was even more aware of inner murmurs tugging at me to go after my dreams. I had studied many philosophies and spiritual disciplines and attended countless personal and business development programs, all with various strategies for making one's life work better. Many of these programs referred to the subject of purpose, but I still hadn't deeply explored the idea for myself. Now I would make the quest for purpose my top priority.

Have you ever wondered if true wealth and finding your purpose in life were pursuits reserved for a lucky few or perhaps they were unrealistic endeavors altogether? As parts of a society, we have been taught to do what we *have* to do and even what we *like* to do, but we have not been trained to concentrate on what we feel *called* to do. When you do only what you have to do, resentment might follow. When you do what you like to do, you may find satisfaction but miss your purpose and the kind of wealth you most desire. However, when you do what you feel *called* to do, something new happens.

As part of my search for clarity, I had once made a collage of sorts. I gathered a bunch of books, pamphlets and magazines related to personal growth and business development. The topics ranged from wealth-building programs to public speaking and motivational seminars. They also included mind-body disciplines, spiritual topics and holistic health and healing. I spread out these resources on my living room floor and declared out loud, "I belong in there somewhere." You can do this same kind of exercise to begin finding your purpose in life and achieving true wealth.

Although Desirée and I had made a lot of money, I did not exactly feel wealthy. As an entrepreneur, what may seem like a lot of money to most people can become consumed during the process of creating the next venture. I also knew deep down that true wealth for me had to do with helping others realize their dreams. Regardless of how much money I was able to make in construction, I knew I would *never* feel wealthy until I found a way to express my deeper passions in the world. I was asking myself the question, How can I create wealth doing what I love while helping other people? I did not know how to get from where I was into a place where I belonged. I thought and thought and thought about this. I could feel my longings, yet nothing changed. I was still trying to *figure out* how I could move forward, but my inner murmurs were defying logic.

What I did not understand was that the process of ordinary logic is often the very obstacle that can prevent clarity and true wealth creation. If you find yourself saying things such as "Yeah, but how does one find clarity and create wealth without figuring it out," you'll be relieved to know that there *is* a way through.

But the goal of wealth creation and finding clarity can seem elusive without the right tools and skills. If your logical mind has not yet led you to wealth and clarity, then most likely it will not. You need to engage an entirely new mechanism, which you will learn more about as you continue reading.

What Is Blocking You?

You must let go, keep letting go,
commit to letting go…
—The Wizard

There was much I had yet to understand, which would come only through experience. To align with your purpose and Wealth Inside Out, it is essential to remove whatever blocks you. First, what blocks you from knowing, and second, what blocks you from taking action? There is tremendous power in removing the blocks that have prevented you from achieving wealth.

I was afraid to begin living my passion because, like many others, I could not envision a way to make it happen. It seemed easier to keep my true wealth desires suppressed; that is, until I came to understand how the mischievous workings of Sneaky Pete (my inner critic and saboteur) were undermining my success and happiness. Only by exploring my intuitive clarity was I able to shift into an effective process that led to my passions in life and what I most wanted. But it did not come about in one fell swoop. There were many obstacles to overcome, mostly the battles in my own mind.

I had been taught that the world works in particular ways, and that to make it in society, one must conform to certain social mores. Like most people, I wanted to fit in. But dreams and goals of the heart do not always fit the way we have been molded. That is where I found myself. I was following ordinary logic, doing what I thought I *had* to do. I wasn't even sure what my real dreams were anymore.

Have you ever followed a path because logically it made good sense, just to find out later that your direction could never fulfill the reasons you went that way in the first place? I see this happen frequently with people who attend wealth building seminars. They may find a good idea for making money but more often than not they are unsuccessful. There are many reasons for this, which we will address throughout the book. Primarily it is because most people do not understand how their thoughts and limiting beliefs are getting in their way. Pay close attention to my story because you will find many parallels that will help you learn how to become successful at wealth creation.

I was unable to see the best options for my true wealth niche until I gave myself permission to step out of the box of my limited thinking. My job now was to distinguish between the dreams and goals of socialized encoding and those of my heart and soul.

I had many fears even though I could feel the tremendous power of what I was tapping into. I was afraid of the unknown and of what others would think. I was afraid of being cast out of my social and family tribe. These seemed like perfectly valid reasons for not wanting to go after my dreams. In fact, they were the very fears that had kept me from even *wanting* to have clarity about how to be successful.

On top of that was my fear of failure. If I failed to reach my goals, would I lose everything I had spent many years working for? Then I would look like a fool. But I also had a fear of success. Fear of success? Why would anyone be afraid of success?

I think I was afraid I would become consumed with more responsibility than I wanted. Looking for any place to direct my fear, I would often question my abilities and my credentials—anything to avoid facing the fact that I was fearful.

Take a look at your own life. Is there something you want that keeps eluding you? What are the circumstances that *seem* to get in your way? Now may be a good time to ask yourself some new questions. Who or what is running your life? Are you going to hide behind your fears or learn how to do what you love and follow your dreams? What are the unwanted beliefs you hold about life, about money, about yourself and what you most want to do? How would you like to turbocharge your ability to now do what you love, create true wealth and overcome your fears?

In reality, the chances of success are on our side. Fear has only the power we ourselves give to it; limiting beliefs can be eliminated and we can learn to create new circumstances. Is your desire for true wealth and happiness strong enough to move you past the obstacles you face? As you consider what's next in your life, really think about what is most important.

Power to Move Forward

When you are clear about your purpose in life, your energy and actions become focused. Fear may not go away completely, but it has less influence in the face of your enormous inner power. When you eliminate the unwanted beliefs that otherwise hold you back, new opportunities come forth. From there, you can start creating new circumstances that lead you toward the kinds of wealth you want. You move forward with confidence.

I liked the idea of moving forward and had already begun to experience this. For example, when I first embarked on authoring *Wealth Inside Out*, I wrote only what seemed important logically. The writing process at that stage felt cumbersome and took a lot of effort. As I went beyond ordinary logic, however, and into the natural wisdom I held inside, the words began to flow with ease.

After much more experience in using my intuitive wealth creation process, I was able to reflect on the precise steps I had taken to move forward. In the next section, you will find fresh perspectives for yourself as I discuss the stages of transition that occurred on the way to finding my purpose in life and Wealth Inside Out. Keep in mind that my personal story is meant to help you understand how each stage may play out. Whenever you see a question that I have asked of myself, that is your cue to ask the same question of yourself.

Six Dimensions of Wealth Creation

The best-educated human being is the one who understands
most about the life in which he [or she] is placed.
—Helen Keller, American author (1880 -1968)

Your path to Wealth Inside Out may require a mutation period, what I call the Six Dimensions of Wealth Creation. The following outline describes the natural transformative process for creating true success and happiness. It is a reliable map—a recipe for success that will help you find your own true wealth direction and your purpose in life (see also Figures 1 and 2).

Your individual journey may begin at any of the six stages because the wealth creation process does not need to occur in any set order. Beginning the quest, however, will often trigger circumstances that bring all of the dimensions into play. Likewise, each step requires deeper layers of understanding and more letting go.

My process began with an ending. Then I asked for inner guidance and clarity, which put me in touch with the rumblings of my lifelong dreams. Then came an elusive stage I call the void. I used this time of uncertainty to clear out limiting beliefs

> One of the first steps toward increasing your wealth creation ability is to understand these stages and identify where you are in the process.

and fears. The more I let go, the more focused I became on what I really wanted to do. I began choosing a new way of life and observed what was also choosing me. All of this was bringing me in touch with my true passion for life and my purpose.

Many others throughout time have set out likewise and were victorious through similar steps in realizing their dreams to find greater joy and abundance, peace of mind, true wealth and sense of purpose. And the way through to *your* unique way of wealth creation and expressing purpose in the world is to invoke life's natural transformative process, which will guide you there. Even more than a recipe for success, the Six Dimensions of Wealth Creation is an *illustration* of the natural phases one usually goes through in finding clarity and creating Wealth Inside Out.

One of the first steps toward increasing your wealth creation ability is to understand these stages and identify where you are in the process. The questions at the end of every section will get you started. We will cover each dimension in greater detail throughout the book. You may also want to boost your success by using the supplementary *Wealth Creation Workbook* discussed on page *i*. You can download this workbook immediately at www.WealthCreationWorkbook.com to further integrate your learning.

1. **Rumblings** — These are deep inner longings or yearnings — the intuitive whispers that call you. You may experience rumblings as a discomfort you can't quite explain or as feelings that seem familiar. Rumblings are primary in sensing your passions in

life and what you really want to do. They give you a greater connection with your calling (if you are willing to pay attention). It is likely that you have been aware of your rumblings throughout life. They prod you to explore further your life purpose and what will bring you true wealth and happiness.

Ask yourself these questions:
When I reflect upon my life experiences, what are the topics of conversation I have most enjoyed? What are the repeating themes that have given me a sense of meaning?

2. **Endings**—Completions occur on two levels, inner and outer. Inner endings are the realization that life the way you have known it is no longer working. You cannot continue down the same road. Outer endings often involve a catalytic life change, such as loss of a job, a health crisis or a divorce. This often takes us by surprise. It is not uncommon for inner endings, our emotional letting go, to lag behind outer endings. In other words, it can take awhile to make the necessary internal transitions to feel complete with an ending.

    When an ending occurs, a new beginning is not always clear even though the time has come for a change. Sometimes it is possible to straddle our current position while creating the new. At other times, we must learn to let go as we find our way forward.

    Both inner and outer endings can initiate a neutral phase I call "the void." This is a fruitful time for generating fresh clarity. The void can also bring up strong emotion or fear, which we address in the next part of the book.

    Ask yourself these questions:
    What ending(s) have occurred in my life that led me to something new and better? What ending(s) have recently occurred where the new beginning may not yet be clear? Is there an ending that needs to happen now in order for me to move forward in my life?

3. **Guidance**—The wisdom of the heart or intuitive knowing is the guidance we seek. Guidance is a secure inner reference place

that helps you reorganize around your true priorities. You can access this inner power by asking for help from the universe, infinite intelligence or simply the part of you that knows. This is not an airy-fairy kind of intelligence, but a clear, inner knowing that has an unmistakable commonsense quality. Receiving clear guidance may require you to surrender to the idea that ordinary ways of functioning so far have failed to put you on your path. To receive guidance, you will need to look inside and ask for help as you let go of how you think the process has to work. As a result, new possibilities and even new realities will emerge; a progression that leads to your heart's desires.

You will also need the guidance of experts to help you become successful. There are many kinds of experts. Some experts will teach you *how* to do what you want to do. Then you need experts who will help you harness the power of self-knowledge and activate the kinds of inner dynamics you need for true success and happiness. You cannot succeed until you have the right thought processes and beliefs in your mind in the right order. Just like you have to program a computer so that 2 x 2 = 4, you must program your mind to receive the kind of wealth you desire. Although I will cover many of the fundamentals in this book on how to do this, you will need the help of experts to gain mastery.

Ask yourself these questions:
Am I willing to consider an easier, more satisfying recipe for success? How can I begin to be in touch with the part of me that knows my true wealth direction? Can I suspend my present beliefs long enough to clarify my true priorities? Am I willing to seek the guidance of expert wealth creation mentors to help me become successful?

4.   **Clearing**—Clearing lets you eliminate the old beliefs and fears that hold you back and tap into the immense inner power you hold at your core. Clearing involves the recalibration of any social conditioning (your internal wiring) that would inhibit your true wealth calling. It is a time for exploring new possibilities, releasing emotional baggage and completing unfinished business.

Clearing could be as simple as cleaning out a closet or garage. Or it may involve changing habitual ways of being, such as adapting new health, diet and exercise regimens. Sometimes you need exposure to new ideas and ways of living to find your way. Some people may even change jobs or social influences. Likewise, important relationships may require new levels of understanding and letting go.

Clearing also involves releasing the need to know how everything will turn out as you learn to trust the process of following your inner guidance. Essentially, clearing helps you get out of your own way so you can achieve the wealth you want.

Ask yourself these questions:
What do I need to let go of to move powerfully toward Wealth Inside Out? What beliefs would I need to have to be in sync with my vision for true success and happiness? Do my relationships support the kind of wealth I want, or do I feel held back?

5. **Choosing**—All the choices you have made up to this point have brought you to an awakening. Choosing requires an honest look at your current level of effectiveness, as well as making new choices that support what you really want to create. It depends upon your commitment not to give up. Keep in mind that new directions usually emerge from a fluid, inner process. Although willpower may be necessary at times to remain on your path, choosing is not so much about forcing as it is about trusting and allowing.

Choosing may involve some critical choice points, yet it is mostly about stepping forward in the face of fear as you learn to fully grasp the enormous strength of your personal inner power. This is a time of installing new positive beliefs that support you in realizing your true wealth dreams. While trusting that life holds a definite place for you, you can more easily step out of the void and into Wealth Inside Out.

Ask yourself these questions:
Is there a time when I made a clear choice and got what I wanted? How did I feel about my triumph? Am I now willing to choose finding my true wealth direction for my next phase of life? Am I willing to make having Wealth Inside Out a priority?

6. **Wealth Inside Out**—Wealth from the inside out includes your purpose and your portfolio of passions. You have a clear direction for your life. Your purpose is what you feel most *called* to express. It is what you were born to do. Your passions encompass all that brings you joy. Your true wealth direction is your primary focus. Wealth Inside Out includes financial, interpersonal, physical and spiritual wealth, and brings you true success and happiness.

When you achieve Wealth Inside Out, you will experience what I call the three C's: clarity, congruence and confidence. Clarity is knowing what you want your life to be about and then moving in a committed direction. Congruence is about matching this inner vision with your outer expression. It is an alignment between your purpose, living your passion and the values you hold dear. Confidence is about being at ease with yourself. That is, you are in touch with the intrinsic significance you bring to life and to other people. I will discuss the three C's in more detail in Chapter Seven.

Wealth Inside Out does not mean that all of your problems will disappear, but they will become less significant. Your focus shifts to your true wealth vision and to how your life matters to others. Wealth Inside Out fulfills the deepest longings of your soul.

Ask yourself these questions:
What are the unique gifts and talents I bring to life and to others? What do I expect to achieve financially, interpersonally, physically and spiritually by finding my purpose in life?

The Void

Somewhere between endings and choosing you may come upon your own journey through the void. This phase usually begins with an ending and ends with a new beginning; however, the void can also occur while traveling through any of the six dimensions. It is a time of incubation, gestation and recalibration that happens naturally whenever any phase of your life is unclear.

This is the stage for which this book ultimately was written. Being in the void often elicits feelings of confusion and uncertainty as one begins to bridge the gap between old ways of being and new understandings that come with Wealth Inside Out.

> You will also need the right tools and skills to keep from getting stuck in the void for long periods.

Some people may even freeze in the void, not knowing how to use the promise of this fruitful time before taking their next steps. What may appear as emptiness is really the way life reorganizes at higher levels. Give yourself enough time in the void so that the reorganization can occur easily.

Not every transition leads to the void. Sometimes changes take place without much uncertainty, but you don't always get to decide how you land. As much as you may try, you can't easily sidestep this process if life has placed you there. One day you'll just recognize that you are in it. Meanwhile, surrender is key to your well-being.

If you find yourself in the void, however, know it is for good reason. The most effective use of your time there is to relinquish your ordinary tendencies and to explore an easier way. This is *not* a good time for planning and goal setting or making big decisions. Goals made in the void often lack clear direction. Your time is best spent with clearing and asking for inner guidance (plus the help of experts), or simply letting things be until you know what to do next.

Fear may tempt you to cling to the past with hopes of reviving what you once had or to shift your focus prematurely toward making plans and goals. You'll have an easier time if you can be present with what is happening naturally.

Think of a baby being born. Life begins with fertilization of the egg, which grows into a fetus, then emerges through various dimensions of development until a new human being is born. You cannot rush this process; it has its own natural timing. However, you can influence the wealth creation process to your benefit when you get the right kind of help.

You also need the right tools and skills to keep from getting stuck in the void for long periods. Armed with the knowledge and skills you will find throughout this book, however, you may need only a few days, weeks or months for this experience. You will know it is over when you begin taking effective action toward your true wealth vision.

As you travel through the Six Dimensions of Wealth Creation, life's natural gestation process may take you through the void. Can you get out of your own way long enough to fulfill your mission—finding your purpose in life and Wealth Inside Out? Remember that letting go, while clearing and asking for help is key.

Ask yourself these questions:
When I am not sure what to do, am I willing to ask for inner and outer help? Am I willing to engage the process of clearing? Am I willing to bask in a peaceful surrender during my time in the void?

Sally's Story

Sally came to us wanting to find clarity about her true wealth vision. We were able to help her by using this powerful process along with some other techniques, which helped her shift her inner dynamics for how to become successful. Sally is one of the nation's leading grant experts, and she was in the void about her direction when we first met. Although she had a sense of what she wanted, clarity came to her using the wealth creation processes we taught her.

Sally had a vision to create a national seminar training company to help others achieve their dreams through grant funding. In less than a year she had catapulted the success of her programs beyond what she had imagined. She later expresses to us; "Before discovering Wealth Inside Out, I felt unclear and fragmented. This was my first step to becoming clear about where I was truly going. I have eliminated the roadblocks to my success. Now I deliver my services nationwide, and people pay me over $50,000 each for my programs. If I can do it using these powerful wealth creation principles, you can too."

I share this story with you for two reasons: First, I want you to get a feel for the power of what is possible once you are clear and have eliminated the roadblocks to *your* success. Sally's business went from near zero to over a million dollars in less than a year. Second, I want you to understand the importance of putting your own priorities in the right order. Just like dialing a friend's phone number, you have to enter the right numbers in the right order. Can you imagine what would happen dialing your set of numbers in a different order? If you missed even one digit will you get what you want?

The same principle applies to creating true wealth and happiness in your life. You need to learn the right program in your mind in the right order to succeed. Finding your purpose in life will get you started, and then knowing what to do and not do in each phase of wealth creation will take you where you want to go.

Figure 1

Six Dimensions of Wealth Creation`

Although displayed here in steps, your individual path may not follow this route exactly. In fact, beginning the quest of Wealth Inside Out often triggers circumstances that bring all the dimensions into play. For example, some people may be in touch with their purpose but need clearing to move forward. Others may need to tune in for guidance or complete an ending before finding clear direction.

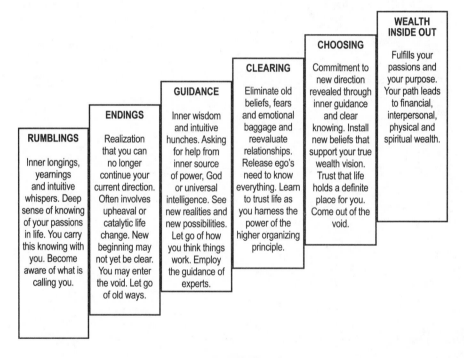

RUMBLINGS

Inner longings, yearnings and intuitive whispers. Deep sense of knowing of your passions in life. You carry this knowing with you. Become aware of what is calling you.

ENDINGS

Realization that you can no longer continue your current direction. Often involves upheaval or catalytic life change. New beginning may not yet be clear. You may enter the void. Let go of old ways.

GUIDANCE

Inner wisdom and intuitive hunches. Asking for help from inner source of power, God or universal intelligence. See new realities and new possibilities. Let go of how you think things work. Employ the guidance of experts.

CLEARING

Eliminate old beliefs, fears and emotional baggage and reevaluate relationships. Release ego's need to know everything. Learn to trust life as you harness the power of the higher organizing principle.

CHOOSING

Commitment to new direction revealed through inner guidance and clear knowing. Install new beliefs that support your true wealth vision. Trust that life holds a definite place for you. Come out of the void.

WEALTH INSIDE OUT

Fulfills your passions and your purpose. Your path leads to financial, interpersonal, physical and spiritual wealth.

The Void

Somewhere between endings and choosing you may come upon a journey to the void. This is a time of gestation, incubation and recalibration. Often it elicits feelings of confusion and uncertainty as you bridge the gap between old ways of being and finding your way. The void is valuable even though it is a time in which nothing seems to be moving. Release old realities and beliefs as new ones are forming during this time. This is *not* a good time for planning or goal setting. Allow clarity to come first through inner guidance and clearing. This natural gestation period will do its job of bringing you to your purpose and Wealth Inside Out.

Figure 2

Finding Your Purpose Through the Six Dimensions

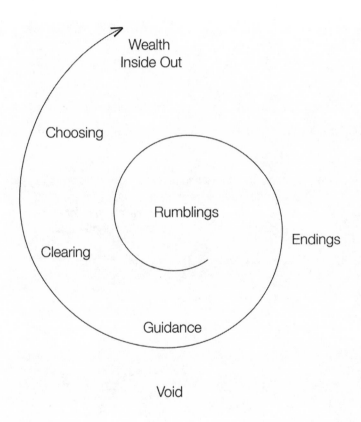

When one door closes another door opens; but we so often look so long and so regretfully upon the closed door, that we do not see the ones which open for us.
—Alexander Graham Bell, Scottish inventor (1847-1922)

Chapter Three

ENDINGS

A Way to Begin Anew

There is a time for departure even when there is no certain place to go.
—Tennessee Williams, American playwright (1911-1983)

Ordinary logic would say to begin with examples of my story from the first dimension, rumblings, before introducing the second dimension, endings. But often we are not aware of our rumblings until we have an ending. Since my journey to Wealth Inside Out was set into motion with an ending, that is where I'll begin. You'll hear about my early rumblings in Chapter Five.

Some endings are planned; others take us by surprise, throwing us into unexpected transition. They range from job losses to health challenges and from relationship changes to spiritual epiphanies. It is always comforting when we are able to plan for an ending. This gives us a sense of control and order; therefore, we can let go more slowly. But many times unforeseen events take place. Planned or unplanned, endings happen to everyone because transition is a natural part of life.

Some endings are planned; others take us by surprise.

Take a moment now to write down some of the pivotal endings from your own life. How did these impact your choices and the direction you took?

Some endings require a purposeful response, which I call surrender or letting go. This does not mean resignation, however. Letting go is not about giving up or losing hope. It is a time to accept things the way they are so something new can begin. Let me give an example in which I learned—the slow way.

Where Did That Come From?

I can't believe the following words came out of my mouth one day: "Asking for help is for weak people who can't think for themselves." Surely I must be more secure than to have made such a statement. Was it actually me thinking this, or was my nemesis Sneaky Pete up to his old tricks? With a hidden belief such as this, how could I possibly ask for help from the universe without seeing myself as weak?

Many people become blocked because they are unwilling to consider something basic to success, such as asking for help. What kinds of beliefs might you have along these lines? Do you ask for help when you need it?

I was disturbed that I was having such thoughts. In fact, I had to know why. I began asking if I felt this way in my heart of hearts, or whether my hidden belief was simply running me. If the latter were true, what other limiting beliefs might be found in the unseen recesses of my mind? And how much influence did these hidden programs have on the outcomes in my life? Just how much control did Ol' Sneaky Pete have over the fact that I hadn't moved toward my true wealth vision, even after exploring the passions I felt so deeply?

Pressure

Choose a job you love, and you will never have to work a day of your life.
— Confucius, Chinese philosopher (551BC-479BC)

As we implemented our grand plans to grow our construction company, I had no clue of the events about to unfold. All of my beliefs about how life works would be challenged. I was sure I had my life figured out, but this next experience would show me just how off track I was.

In the past, my drive for achievement had sometimes overpowered my effectiveness. In the case of our financial goals, we had made substantial headway, but the path we were on was no longer working. I could feel the pressure of our situation, but I knew deep down I would not continue building. When I thought about working in the old way, I felt my spirit was dying inside. I wanted to make money doing work I loved, but it seemed Sneaky Pete was having greater success. I was not yet connected with my Wizard and the voice of higher wisdom that would help me find true success and happiness.

Take a look at your own life. Have you ever continued in a direction that needed to change—a relationship, a job or some kind of involvement that you felt was over?

Continuing anyway, Desirée and I created a company mission statement to reflect our sense of purpose: *We Are Custom Residential Builders, Dedicated to Building Your Dream.* The second part of this statement spoke to me deeply, and I thought it would help me shift to feel aligned with my purpose in life. This might have worked had I still had enough juice for construction. But I was only deceiving myself and, in turn, had lost track of my true needs.

Construction had been an important step in my journey; I enjoyed many aspects of the work and always did a good job for clients. But I was done. This was the beginning of my ending and the doorway to the elusive state of being I call the void (Figure 1). Now I was living in the neutral time between an ending and a new beginning that was not yet clear.

Awakenings

Destiny is what you were supposed to do in life.
Fate is what kicks you in the ass to make yourself do it.
—Henry Miller, American author (1891-1980)

Over the previous several months as we planned to expand our construction company, I noticed a fluttering sensation in my head when I was sleeping. It would wake me up several times each night. At first I didn't think much about it, believing it was just tension. However, the closer we came to landing a new contract, the more intense the fluttering, and I became concerned.

This was about the time that my heart began racing, and I thought my life might be over. As I stood clinging to the back of the sofa that day, Desirée came running, and off we went to the local hospital. Of course I was very nervous, but the doctors didn't appear too concerned. They acted like nothing much was going on as I got on the table. I thought maybe this is just the way they are trained to help calm their patients. Next, I was hooked to a matrix of wires and gadgetry that seemed from another planet. All I could do was lie there talking with Desirée and our friend Kipra, who came to be with us. A couple of hours later, the doctor walked in smiling and said, "Your heart seems fine. Perhaps you are just stressed out and need to slow down and take it easy."

Shaken by this experience, I followed up with several doctors, including a cardiologist. After a long battery of tests, my physicians were not coming up with anything conclusive. I was perplexed because I knew something was off, yet everyone was telling me I was fine. I had no idea what I would do next.

Months elapsed without resolution; I was ready for an entirely different approach, even something unconventional. I had heard about several medical intuitives who could tell what was going on in the mind-body relationship through what is known as an "energy reading." These intuitives often supplement medical tests and procedures by perceiving subtle, underlying stress patterns that might be causing one's condition.

I learned about the work of Dr. Norman Shealy, a Harvard-trained neurosurgeon who had been working with intuitives for many years. As an avid researcher, Dr. Shealy found that some intuitives could diagnose his patients with an 80% rate of accuracy. One in particular he found to be 93% accurate for both physical and psychological conditions.

Faithe Socorro had been in traditional health care for many years prior to her full-time practice as a medical intuitive. During her career, she often could tell the prognosis before laboratory tests were run. Although I did not distinguish her level of accuracy, I trusted the referral and decided to give her a call.

During our first session over the telephone, Faithe began by asking what I wanted to find out, and I told her of my health concerns. Then she explained the rationale of her work, which was not completely unfamiliar because of my lifelong studies in several mind-body disciplines.

Our conversation went something like this: "I am going to tell you how disease works on a subconscious level," Faithe said. "Illness comes into your energy body first. During this phase, you feel symptoms that may not yet show up on tests of Western medicine. This can make you feel kind of crazy because you know something is going on that is not being verified. However, if you do not deal with what the symptoms are trying to tell you, they can later manifest in the body as illness."

Her initial comments brought some degree of relief. I felt validated for what I was experiencing. She continued, "Your physical body is not what concerns me the most. What is going on has to do with your finances and what you do for a living. Tell me about your work."

Now this is not anything I expected to hear in a medical reading, but I was intrigued. Something rang true about what she was saying.

I told Faithe of our plans to grow our construction company and sell it in five years. I went on to say that I actually wanted out of this business and was trying to find a new way of wealth creation in a field I enjoy. However, I had resigned myself to the idea that the best way to achieve my goal was to make our existing business more successful and then sell it.

Her response was gentle but firm. "I'm sure you have a good plan and have invested a lot of time and money. But if you keep going, it will probably kill you."

This got my attention.

She went on. "You're draining your energy, and for long enough that you have become depleted."

She explained that everything we do either supplies energy or drains us. If we no longer enjoy what we are doing, we lose energy. This in turn lowers our body's resistance to illness. Could this be what was happening to me? Everything I once believed about medicine and cures was now up for question.

As I reached for some rational order, she asked a most unexpected question. "What would you *really* like to do?"

I said, "You know, I'm not even sure anymore. I think I'd like to take a year off to reorient my life."

"Do you have a way to do that?" she asked.

"Well, not realistically. At least I couldn't without backsliding financially. I need to pay my bills and put food on the table and create wealth for the future."

I told her about the apartment units we owned in Oklahoma City and that we planned to accumulate a large portfolio of properties until we had enough units for a more passive cash flow. I said that this was something I enjoyed.

She responded, "Well, if you have to continue construction to pay your bills, you had better find a way to make it fun. And you'd best get done with it in the next year or so. By the way," she added, "I don't see this whole real estate idea happening, either."

I reacted intensely. "What do you mean? You don't understand. We've enjoyed our work in real estate, and we have a viable strategy that will bring financial freedom."

"Well, you may have that one deal going, but when I hear you talk about it, I don't hear your resonance for real estate as a primary passion," she said, not letting up. "You are doing it only for the money, and this alone will not sustain you."

"Yeah, but we have such a good plan, and I'm sure it will work," I protested.

"If that is what you wanted to do with your life, you wouldn't feel so off course. You would immerse yourself in this direction with total passion for life and a sense of purpose," she countered. "Sure you might succeed, but what will it cost in terms of your health and peace of mind? What kind of wealth is that?"

We talked back and forth like this for a while, mostly with me reacting to her observations and trying to push the merits of our plan. She held firm on what she was picking up from me. She was reading my energy, not my words.

"When a person talks," she said, "one's tone of voice, body language and energy are broadcasting what is actually going on internally, regardless of the words." She explained that what a person broadcasts either resonates with what they are saying or it doesn't. There's no negotiating this resonance. One either has congruence with what they are doing or not. No one can fake it.

To myself, however, I was thinking, "Well okay, maybe I don't have all the right answers, even though it sure seems like I have some good ones... I mean, after all, I'm pretty smart and usually figure things out. And besides, if *I* think of it, surely it must be an okay solution." My internal monolog continued, "Faithe doesn't understand that I've spent more than 25 years developing my knowledge and skills and learning how to be successful. I already know a lot about life and well-being. And what about all the trainings I've attended on inner development, personal growth and business success, learning about how things work in the real world? And besides, I've been pretty successful...."

After a few moments of my silence, Faithe said, "Mark, you have a well-developed mind, but right now it's getting in the way of what you want."

New Possibilities

You must trust yourself even as you lean on the sustaining power of the infinite, for it is through your inner self alone that this infinite becomes realized and manifested in your experience.
— Ernest Holmes, American spiritual writer (1880-1960)

Again, what Faithe had said struck a chord. If I truly had all these things figured out, why was my life not working? My cash flow was backsliding, my health was going downhill, I was not doing work I loved and I couldn't seem to put my life together with a sense of flow and balance. Okay, I concluded, maybe it was time to consider another way.

"What would you *really* like to do?" she repeated.

"You know, just like I said before, I don't even know anymore. I've spent much of my life trying to figure this out, but all of my planning and logic doesn't seem to be getting me where I want to be."

"Do you ever ask for guidance?"

"Uh, guidance?"

"Yes, that's right, guidance," she said emphatically.

"Uh, I don't think in the way that you're talking about," I confessed.

"Well, that's your homework, to ask for guidance." Then she gave me an exercise designed to rewire the neural receptors in the brain while saying the words *It is safe to receive guidance.*

You can learn to do this same exercise yourself by following the instructions provided in the *Wealth Creation Workbook* discussed on page i.

I got off the phone feeling uneasy, confused, and frankly, quite upset. Who the heck is she to tell me how my life is and what works and what doesn't? At the same time, some of what she said rang true.

In a daze, I continued sorting out the truth about my situation while remembering all that Faithe had said.

Sneaky Pete was having a field day with my medical intuitive reading. He was laughing and making remarks like, "Whatever gave you the idea to talk to a psychic? Those kinds of people are weird, don't you think? Oh wow, let me read your aura. I can feel the vibrations of your chakras communicating with me, man. Let me tell you what's going on with your energy."

"Oh, shut up," I silenced Sneaky Pete. "Can't you see my ordinary way isn't working?"

Recognizing I was at a dead end, I decided to do my little brain rewiring exercise for the next couple of weeks while I sorted out my situation. I really didn't think it would work, and just as Sneaky Pete had suspected, nothing new was happening anyway.

Inner and Outer Endings

As I grappled with Faithe's observations, I wondered what would come next. One thing for sure, something had begun to shift. Now I was learning firsthand about the void and about endings. I experienced two kinds of endings, both inner and outer.

> Have you ever had an experience where the time had come for change and you had no idea what to do next?

Remember, the changes that occur in our everyday circumstances, such as financial loss, divorce, getting fired and so forth, are outer endings. As for me, I had experienced a sudden dip in health, lost my drive to continue down the path I was on and ended my construction career. These were my outer endings.

Inner endings are about the internal process of dealing with change. In my confusion, all I knew was that I was no longer willing to do anything that did not feel energizing. It took me a while, however, to come to terms with what was happening.

When something ends, it is often difficult to accept what seems like a loss. I was so used to *making* things happen that it wasn't an easy transition. At first, I would cling to the way things were. When that didn't work, I'd try to push myself forward by making new plans and goals. Again, I was trying to make something happen while lacking real clarity.

Outer circumstances are not the only trigger for inner endings. Sometimes we *know* it is time for a change and can begin a more planned transition. I had attempted this but kept having difficulties. Now it seemed that life was taking me down an entirely new path, one that required me to let go of other agendas.

Maybe if I continued asking for guidance and clarity, something new would occur. I decided to give this idea a fair try. Take a look into your own life. Have you ever had an experience where the time had come for change and you had no idea what to do next?

Jerry's Story

Jerry came to us and wanted to feel more at ease with his life direction and in his relationships. He had made a lot of money in business and enjoyed helping other people. However, he felt that people often took advantage of his generosity. He was never quite sure if his friends and family wanted his friendship or only his money. Jerry was often afraid to say no to people who were close to him, yet he often felt drained by certain people. He thought maybe if he said no to a request, that he would lose a friendship and connection.

Desirée and I helped Jerry eliminate several "negative" self-esteem beliefs that were getting in his way. One of the hidden beliefs that Jerry eliminated was *What makes me good enough and important is helping other people in need.* In other words, Jerry had a hard time seeing his own goodness unless he was helping someone in need. Giving money to his friends and family made him *feel* important, but deep down he was not truly in touch with that. Jerry decided to elicit an ending and stop giving his money so indiscriminately. Before long, he was giving only when he felt it was truly warranted and he no longer felt mowed over.

Jerry began to enjoy his money more freely, as he could now focus more easily on the things that made him feel fulfilled and happy. He began to get involved in projects that gave him a truer sense of belonging. Using his wealth of business experience, which had made him successful financially, Jerry began helping people create success in their businesses. The ending of a single unwanted habit had led him to focus on what he most valued.

Endings

Points to Remember

- Some endings are planned, others unplanned. Either way, we enter a time of transition when we leave the old behind.

- Endings sometimes take us by surprise with upheaval or a catalytic life-change, dropping us suddenly into the void.

- The void is a fruitful time of incubation and recalibration. Remember that endings often occur before a new beginning is clear. Trying to bypass the void will not usually lead you in a clear and confident direction.

- Endings reveal themselves when we know on some level that we cannot continue on our current path.

- Open yourself to new possibilities and new ways of thinking. This makes your endings easier to handle.

- Pay attention to both inner and outer endings and what life is trying to communicate through your endings.

- As you face the reality of an ending, the key is letting go. If you stop trying to control specific outcomes long enough, you can begin to get in sync with your true wealth vision and what you most desire.

- Whenever you experience an ending, ask for inner guidance and clarity through your intuitive knowing, which will naturally lead you to what is next.

For more powerful exercises about endings that will help you achieve wealth from the inside out, download your supplementary *Wealth Creation Workbook* at www.WealthCreationWorkbook.com.

Chapter Four

GUIDANCE

Opening New Doors

*We grow by following some divine interior awareness,
which was implanted in us before time began.*
—Ernest Holmes, American spiritual writer (1880-1960)

Since ordinary logic had failed to put me on my path, I was ready for something new. Meanwhile, what began as a simple exercise opened up a new way to look at my situation.

I learned that inner guidance may come in many forms, from intuitive hunches and premonitions to just knowing. It can also come through dreams and streaming thoughts. It could even be as simple as a sudden flash of insight. Yet, several hurdles may appear when we invite guidance into our lives. For instance, will we have the willingness to trust the clarity within us? Will we follow what it says?

Learning to interpret the messages of inner guidance can seem daunting at first. Some messages are literal and others are symbolic, leaving us with the job of sorting out which is which. In addition, internal messages can become muddled by unhealed emotional baggage rife with the desires of ego.

This is where clearing comes into play and we see why it is so vital. You can begin to find what inside you is truly looking for expression by simply stepping *toward* your inner callings while clearing out your limiting beliefs and thoughts. This is the *process* that will lead you to clarity and to Wealth Inside Out.

When first learning about the process of inner clarity, you must also learn to discern between impulse and clear knowing. Momentary passion without clarity can lead you off your path. So it is important to identify your real desires. Moreover, clarity may require that you expand your knowledge in whatever direction you are pursuing. For example, think of a new relationship. Impulse may lead you to get involved with others who do not share your same values. However, when you learn effective relationship skills, you will ask questions and pay attention to the way a person affects you. In this same way, intuitive perception may lead you in a new direction where you will also need to gain new knowledge and skills before clarity grabs hold. This is why you will also need the guidance of experts in their respective fields, a matter which I will address in the next section.

This took me a while to grasp. I had lots to learn about following my inner compass and about surrender. Letting go to follow what we feel called to express does not mean we can't have our ordinary dreams and goals, but the quest for purpose and Wealth Inside Out becomes our first priority. Although some people have done well on a conventional path, this seems to work best only when everyday plans and goals lead to a truly desired place. Making such plans and goals had been working for me in many ways, but I never felt that I was on my right path. Now, I began to explore what intuitive guidance—a different method—was all about.

At first, some people have difficulty with the idea of guidance. One way to get more comfortable with the process is to see it as gaining inner wisdom and improved mental clarity. But be careful. Often when we feel stuck, it is because we are blocking the truth in a situation. We can lose clarity by wanting to control outcomes that may not be congruent with our innermost clarity. So the question is Does your discomfort come from trying a new method or is it more from hidden fear?

Following guidance and intuitive clarity helps you resolve the ongoing conflict between what you are currently doing and the true wealth direction you honestly want to follow. In my case, I was trained to believe you had to take charge and make things happen. In one sense, this is true. But if you avoid the wisdom of your heart and what you most value, life will become one big struggle. The guidance of your inner wisdom will open new portals of opportunity, which is about receiving the wonderful possibilities life already has for you.

Many Forms of Guidance

The mind can assert anything and pretend it has proved it.
My beliefs I test on my body, on my intuitional consciousness,
and when I get a response there, then I accept.
—David Herbert Lawrence, English writer (1885-1930)

The wisdom of inner guidance communicates through ordinary physiological avenues. Some of us find clarity through gut instinct, for example. We experience a body sensation that gives us a sense of knowing. Another way is through intuitive hunches or unexplainable urges as we feel our way along.

A lot of my clarity comes through a silent inner voice. Words that are strong, clear and concise come to my mind without me having to think or reason. Others find clarity through a simple inner knowing. "I just know," they may say with conviction without being able to tell you how.

Some people see pictures, either still images or miniature movies in their mind's eye. Clarity may also try to reach you through your dreams. There is less resistance when we are sleeping, so become aware of your dreams and what they may be trying to tell you.

Many of us gain knowledge through *all* the physical senses—touch, taste, sound, smell and sight. When we simply tune in, our particular way of understanding this inner technology will reveal itself. As you begin using this powerful tool for self-understanding and direction, you'll likely find that your senses become heightened, which gives you greater ability to recognize the true wealth rumblings that are seeking expression from within you.

Guidance of Experts

Regardless of whatever direction you pursue, you need skilled people who can help you learn how to become successful. There are many kinds of experts. There are subject matter experts who will teach you facts and theories about a field of study. Often these are the kinds of experts you find in a traditional educational setting. Although they may teach about a subject, in many cases, they do not actually practice what they know in real world applications. Then there are accomplished experts who will teach you the practical, hands-on skills you need to know. These kinds of people most often have applied real world experience and have achieved great success in their given fields.

You can learn a lot from both of these kinds of experts, but there is another kind of expert that often goes overlooked, yet is probably the most vital. Working with this kind of expert may in fact determine your success. I am talking about people who will help you *integrate* all that you have learned so that you can finally achieve the wealth and happiness you deserve. I sometimes call these people wealth catalysts or wealth mentors, as they help you harness your deepest passions and turn them into wealth. You need to know how to make the *inner* changes necessary for success in any area of your life. Your wealth mentor will help you make those changes to achieve financial, interpersonal, physical or spiritual success. Take a moment right now to think about who you could begin seeking out to mentor you in these various ways.

One time while working with Tomiko (one of our wealth mentoring students) I could see that she really *wanted* to be successful at wealth creation, and she had attended several seminars about how to do this. Like many others, Tomiko did not yet understand that you have to go beyond learning facts, figures and strategies. First, you need a clear focused vision for living your passion and learning how to do what you love. You need make sure that what you do for money fits with your unique wealth personality. Then you need to have wealth creation confidence. Tomiko had gained the *knowledge* to create wealth, but that wasn't enough.

First we helped Tomiko find her passion and learn how to make money doing what she loved. Then using one of our powerful wealth creation processes we helped Tomiko eliminate hidden beliefs such as "Money is scarce and hard to get," "I can't make money doing what I love," "I'm not capable," and "I don't have what it takes," along with a few others. Can you imagine trying to create wealth if you believe that money is scarce and hard to get? Unfortunately, nearly all people have at least some of these kinds of limiting beliefs hidden in their subconcious.

The good news is that there is an easy way to identify these wealth destroying gremlins and eliminate them, a matter which I will address in Chapter Six.

Only after we helped Tomiko *integrate* all that she had learned about wealth creation did she find true success and happiness. She learned how to make the inner changes necessary to become successful.

Regardless of your wealth creation direction, you need skilled people who can help you. Whether you want financial, interpersonal, physical or spiritual wealth, you will need the guidance of experts who can help you learn how to finally achieve the wealth and happiness you desire.

Dare to Dream

The efforts which we make to escape from
our destiny only serve to lead us into it.
— Ralph Waldo Emerson, American essayist and poet (1803-1882)

One morning about two weeks after my medical intuitive reading, Desirée and I lay in bed talking about our dreams and hopes for the future. "If we were to begin a new direction together, what would we really like to do?" I asked. "Let's imagine we just got out of high school, only we have the benefit of our existing knowledge and life experience."

We imagined there were no obstacles or concerns about money. We got to create the life we wanted—and it was guaranteed to happen. Now that was exciting. Sneaky Pete didn't have a chance in that conversation. He couldn't get two words in edgewise. We were having too much fun letting our imaginations run free.

You can do this same process of visioning without limitations whenever you want to get in touch with your deeper passion for life. This is a well-founded process that has worked for many people.

Desirée and I began to talk about developing a retreat center where teachers, trainers, business leaders and healers would come to deliver their workshops and seminar programs. We elaborated about the fun we would have being immersed in the personal development world. We could create a tranquil campus environment that enveloped a sense of the sacred. The programs would inspire people and give them the skills and knowledge to achieve true success and happiness and to understand the many kinds of wealth creation. We envisioned state-of-the-art seminar rooms, a spa facility, delicious dining, body movement programs and a community room. This would be a wonderful, expansive place that people would recognize as special.

A while later, we got up to do our morning breathing practice, a 20-minute yoga routine. This practice has always put me in a calm state of mind, yet after my breathing that morning, something new happened. Out of the stillness, I began to sense a realm of awareness beyond ordinary thinking. And it related to the retreat center.

This is the correct direction. You can begin now with your upcoming trip. Go to Feathered Pipe Ranch in Montana and The Crossings in Texas. These places will help you expand your vision and understand what is needed to assemble your business plan.

Wow! This was interesting! Was I receiving guidance like Faithe had talked about? Or was I just making up stuff in my head? I do know this: Something about this experience was different from anything I had known. It seemed real, yet I kept thinking, "How can this be?" It was like hearing another voice, only it made no sound. But the words were clear and concise, and somehow comforting.

I ran into the next room to tell Desirée what had happened, and she immediately shared in my curiosity. Then I asked her pointedly, "Do you really want to do the retreat center?"

Almost instantly she said, "Yes," and we both began to feel a sense of clarity and calm.

Breathing and meditation are not the only ways to access inner clarity, but you will need to find a way to turn off the chatter of your mind long enough to find stillness. When you enter a place of silence and ask for help, you unlock the gateway to your subconscious mind and your intuitive perception. This gives you access to the part of your brain that is beyond ordinary logic. You may also find this kind of stillness when walking, gardening or taking a bath; however, you can ask for inner guidance and clarity anytime, anywhere. Just ask and listen.

Later that day, while getting a massage, I settled into the deep semiconscious state that often happens during bodywork. Then guidance appeared again.

This is your soul's purpose. All that you need will be given to you.

I couldn't quite grasp what was happening. *This is your soul's purpose* was a strong message indeed. The words kept reverberating in my mind throughout the rest of the day.

The next morning, I sat for meditation, not sure what would happen. Would I receive more guidance, or had I had a fleeting, one-time experience?

I decided to stretch myself even further and actually ask for guidance. I tried different ways of communicating with the part of me that was presenting answers.

Again, I did something unconventional. I said the following words aloud:

O Great Spirit,
come to me
work through me

And then guidance came again.

You may create your vision and mission for the retreat center.

"What is the mission?" I asked the silent voice.

A sacred, playful healing place to connect with spirit, community and your purpose for living. From there you can build your true wealth dreams.

This was where our organizational training began to pay off. We had learned a method for writing out our vision and mission statements. Right then and there, I sat and wrote the first draft of our vision, mission and values (Figure 3). It flowed out almost effortlessly.

The process of identifying and writing your own vision, mission and values is beyond the scope of this book; however, it is an effective method of pinpointing the prime elements of clarity. You can begin by using the draft on the following page as a template to further define your own vision.

Essentially, your vision is a snapshot of what you see for a meaningful future. Your mission is similar to your purpose, which reflects the gifts you bring to others. Typically, a mission statement is used in business and a purpose statement is used for discovering personal clarity. Your core values represent the fundamental principles you live by.

I must note that also important to my wealth creation process was journaling the messages of inner guidance so that I could later reflect on what had been expressed. This is how I recaptured the dynamic wisdom I was receiving so I could share it with others.

> You may find it helpful to use the supplemental *Wealth Creation Workbook* referenced at the beginning of this book, or attend one of our Wealth Inside Out™ training programs to further increase your wealth creation ability.

Figure 3

Kamuela Holistic Resort™
(Kah-moo-wael-la)

D – R – A – F – T

Our Vision
A distinctive educational retreat center on the Big Island, Hawaii. We are recognized for

- Our outstanding workshops, trainings and retreats for personal and business development, which are led by pioneering teachers and leaders from around the world.

- Our tranquil retreat campus, which is architecturally intermingled with the natural surroundings.

- Our omnipresent sense of community, which people carry back to their own communities.

Mission / Purpose
Our mission is to inspire individuals and business leaders to know their purpose, realize their potential and live out their vision and dreams in a way that supports a larger good.

Values / Ideals
- Serving as an educational enhancement to local and global communities.

- Conducting all activities responsibly and with integrity.

- Cultivating leadership that inspires the human spirit and transforms lives.

- Fostering success through inner development and harmonious relationships.

Suddenly, Sneaky Pete began to work me pretty hard. I became confused and wondered if I were losing my mind. On the one hand, the inner guidance seemed real and natural. On the other hand, there was no logical sense in it. Where were the messages coming from? I still feared I was just making stuff up. Was there a part of my psyche I had never accessed before? Or was some greater intelligence in the universe communicating with me?

A few days later, I asked for guidance and clarity again. "Please confirm the direction of our retreat center. And quite frankly, when will we get some relief regarding our income and cash flow?"

You will locate on the north end of the Big Island of Hawaii. It will be a destination retreat center. As you explore other retreat centers, the scale and model will become clear. You will be building something that is very unique and unlike any other. Don't worry about your cash flow and income. It will be remedied soon. You can spend your time healing and resting while you gather what you need to clarify your vision.

Desirée and I looked at a map of Hawaii and saw the little town of Waimea, also known as Kamuela (Kah-moo-wael-la). We had been there once before during our first trip to Hawaii and we both liked the small-town feel of it. Somewhere nearby, we had thought, is where we would like to live. That is how we had come up with the name, Kamuela Holistic Resort. We had no idea what *Kamuela* meant; we just liked the name and went with it. But during the months ahead, we had often wondered if the name held any special significance.

I was excited about our retreat center, but as I expanded into this vision I kept feeling overwhelmed and even more confused. I wasn't sure about getting involved in such a big undertaking. Yet, the idea of retreats seemed so familiar, and I was stimulated by the inner messages during my still moments. I found the process fascinating even though I was stirred up. I really had no frame of reference for what was happening.

> Keep asking for guidance and clarity until you get what seems like clear counsel in your subconscious.

I knew only to continue asking for help while clearing the limitations in my mind. My quest to comprehend the changes is what led me to create the Six Dimensions of Wealth Creation. If you find yourself feeling confused at any point, you can refer to the map of this process in Figures 1 and 2 to regain your bearings. Keep asking for guidance and clarity until you get what seems like clear counsel in your subconscious. Then begin taking action while reaching for greater understanding.

Over those same few days, nothing happened after my breathing practice, so I continued experimenting with the process. I wanted to explore the idea that indeed some higher source of knowledge or intuitive knowing was helping me align with my life purpose.

I would say things such as "I release all thoughts and beliefs that do not fully support who I am and my highest good." And, "I ask for clarity as I go about each day... I allow myself to harmonize with the natural flow of life as I move forward with ease and confidence."

"Come on, don't cop out on me now," I joked to this invisible source of the messages. "I'm beginning to warm up to this guidance idea. Please talk to me again. I'll try to listen better."

This went on for about four days with Sneaky Pete chiming in to sabotage me. "Mark, you have certainly lost your marbles to think that you can get anywhere in life with this nonsense."

Striving for Clarity

Man's mind stretched to a new idea never
goes back to its original dimensions.
— Oliver Wendell Holmes, American jurist (1841-1935)

Finally, guidance came again.

There is no reason to be unclear. That only comes from fear. When you surrender to the natural flow of life, it is easy to know where you want to go. There is no doubt that a retreat center is the direction you need to go. However, you must choose your path anew each and every day.

I began to notice that whenever I was in my clear state of mind, the messages about the retreat center felt certain. Later, when I would think too much, my fear would resurface. Sneaky Pete was, of course, no help. He loved to play on my fears. This back and forth went on for quite a while before I eventually became comfortable with the process.

It would be even longer before I understood the particular ways in which I would work in the world.

I could see my progress at each phase of the journey, and you will note your progress as well. Don't give up because of the discomfort you may encounter along the way. Your strong desire will keep you stepping toward your true wealth dreams with ever greater clarity and focus. You may also find it helpful to pay attention to the inner messages I found for myself. Do you notice any parallels that may apply in your life?

I began to observe that when I was not afraid, I was excited, very excited. I was just not sure what form the messages about retreats would take. All I could see were new kinds of thoughts moving through my mind as I remained skeptical.

I had always felt connected with the unseen aspects of life, but I had more to understand. Although I was raised to some extent in the tradition of the Episcopal Church, the primary influences in my life have been more secular—and ones that are inclusive of universal principles, the mind-body connection and a deep respect for personal sovereignty.

I'm a little embarrassed to admit this, but I realized through my new experiences that I had often viewed what lies beyond the physical as something like entertainment. Now I was having direct experience with the spiritual nature of life, and the teachings began to sink in on an entirely new level.

> Don't give up because of the discomfort you may encounter along the way. Your strong desire will keep you stepping toward your true wealth dreams.

This inspired me to reach deeper to find truth. I realized that each person's view of reality is only one paradigm, one he or she has come to believe. I needed to find a way that worked for me, and this is what I set out to do. Most of all, I wanted my life filled with the kind of inner wealth and happiness that comes from being clear. If asking for guidance would lead me there, I was game. I had let Sneaky Pete hold me back long enough.

I continued experimenting with different ways of asking for guidance about finding my purpose in life. Not much else seemed important.

> Infinite guidance,
> please show me the way to my true calling in life.
> I want to know my higher purpose and my passion.
> Please show me the way to align with my life mission
> in every way—spiritually, emotionally,
> financially and otherwise.
> Please help me find
> true wealth and happiness.

And a response came for me.

It is important to take time for reflection and deep rest. From there, wholeness and balance will come. Keep practicing your breathing and meditation every day. Try not to let yourself worry during this time. The true success and happiness you are seeking will come.

Keep in mind there is no prescribed way of asking for inner guidance. You can use the verse above and the others throughout the book as a way to begin. Try saying your requests for help out loud, and with all sincerity.

Permission to Explore

Imagination is the true magic carpet.
— Norman Vincent Peale, American clergyman (1898-1993)

At this point, I began to engage somewhat conversationally with the part of me that was offering answers. Whether or not this voice was a divine presence or the thoughts of my subconscious mind, there was something authentic about it that made me feel connected. It almost seemed as though the inner messages were embedded deep within me since before I was even born. For a while, I grappled with what to call the voice. I wrote out names such as higher power, infinite wisdom, God and so on.

You'll recall from Chapter One that my experience was like having an intelligent wizard inside who spoke to me from the infinite. So I began to call the voice *Wizard,* which allowed me to engage in these conversations with a sense of fun. Through the Wizard, I had a liaison between the infinite source and myself. I could talk with my Wizard all I wanted, and no one else would even have to know about it.

I explained to the Wizard that I kept having thoughts about coaching, teaching and training. I said that although I enjoyed teaching others how to become successful, I was not clear of my role and how all this fit into the big picture. I wondered how this would affect my time in relation to developing a retreat center.

Then I said, "Please, Wizard, help me understand what to do."

Keep letting go. Stop trying to remember every detail as you continue to focus on balance. The answers you need will come.

Talking with the Wizard helped somewhat, but even so, my ordinary logic kept getting in the way. I think nearly all of us grapple with being open to new ideas when we don't understand something. In fact, it is common to become critical in such instances. But I simply had to find out what was happening, which required that I allow myself permission to explore.

I went to a large bookstore to see what books I could find on the topic of inner guidance. I wanted to know what others with similar experiences had discovered about pursuing this process in the face of fear.

I learned about many viewpoints, from heart intelligence to talking with angels and from quantum physics to the subconscious mind. I read about chakras and guidance, medical intuitives, life transition, wealth creation and clearing out limiting beliefs. All of these resources were helpful and further confirmed the way people explain life according to his or her particular beliefs. Now, I was ready for a way to relate to my experience that I could fully embrace.

Where I grew up, talking about chakras and guidance would seem kind of nutty, as Sneaky Pete reminded me daily. Yet, many people find tremendous clarity this way. In spite of all my exploration, however, I remained confused and needed some practical grounding. I kept asking for more clarity and understanding.

Dream Guidance

Infinite
intelligence,
creator of all things,
I ask for your continued guidance daily.
Please direct me on my true wealth path.
Please show me the way.

Continue letting go of effort. Keep surrendering. Be in peace as you learn to trust. Know that what you need will come.

The next three nights, I had five powerful and prophetic dreams. Two dreams came the first night. In dream number one, I had a mouthful of chewing gum that was choking me. As I pulled the gum out of my mouth, it stretched and I had to keep pulling to get it unstuck from my throat. The throat, I learned from studying dream interpretation, represents the fifth chakra or energy center of the body, which is the source of communication and the voice of creative expression. Gum has to do with something sticky. What came to me from this dream was that pulling the gum out of my throat was symbolic of unblocking my communication and self-expression.

In the second dream, I was swimming to the mainland from an island. The waves were huge, yet I remained in control as I swam with equal energy and power. I could navigate the swells and troughs in such a way that I was pulled forward with vast speed and growing momentum. Other people were swimming too, and I passed them all. Eventually, I came to a bridge, got out of the water and crossed the bridge to the docks. The bridge was constructed of a transparent, poly-type fabric, so I could see through to the water below. I walked along the docks to my car. Next, I was flying in a helicopter with several of my friends, showing them where I had begun the dream on the island.

The dream left me feeling energized and free from the restraints of my past. I could now move forward in my life.

In the next couple of dreams, I released some deep sobs of grief and worked through some additional blocks in my thinking.

The third night, I dreamed about the subject of finding your purpose in life and putting together wealth creation retreats in Hawaii.

These dreams shook me to my core. I was unsure of what would become of my vision, but I could not turn back. I still had a long way to go.

I looked forward to being involved in success development programs and helping people create wealth and improve the quality of their lives. I made another request:

Infinite mind,
Please remove my confusion.
Help me clarify what to do each day.
Help me remove the obstacles that are in my way.
Please help me release and
let go of anything that is blocking me.
Help me reach true success in my career,
doing work I love and enjoy.
Please show me how to create
true wealth and happiness and
satisfy my deepest longings.

You can see my difficulty. I would ask for guidance, receive answers and then not trust what I was hearing. I could not seem to separate the inner guidance from my fears and the voice of Sneaky Pete. I would often shift back into planning and drive to *feel* secure, but pushing against the flow only wore me down. At times, it even made me sick.

I reread my wealth creation journal and typed up only the guidance portions to examine their sequence. Through this process, I realized my need to surrender at yet another level. I could focus on my new forms of insight or continue to dwell on my fear. This was my choice. Who would I listen to, Sneaky Pete or the Wizard?

I began to notice that whenever I focused on my distress, I felt lousy. When I tuned into the guidance, I felt good. It would take the experiences of the next several months to integrate what was happening and to follow my instincts without hesitation and confusion.

You may consider starting your own wealth creation journal by writing down what comes to you whenever you ask for guidance and clarity. Pay attention to your reactions as you find the voice of your own inner wisdom.

Talking With Nature

There was a time when humanity recognized itself as part of nature....
— Ted Andrews, author of Animal Speak (1952-)

A few weeks later, Desirée and I went to Helena, Montana for a one-week yoga retreat at the Feathered Pipe Ranch, where I had often vacationed over the past 17 years. Being at Feathered Pipe is like going off to summer camp, only for adults. One of the other participants called it "adult daycare." A typical day involves a couple of two-hour yoga classes followed by delicious meals, leisurely walks in the woods, massages, afternoon naps and plenty of camaraderie. It is not a fancy place like the ones at extravagant spas, but being there has always met my needs for rejuvenation and time for reflection. Some of the sleeping accommodations are in tent-like cabins known as yurts, which are situated in the middle of a beautiful pine forest. The stillness at Feathered Pipe is remarkable. There is no other place quite like it.

> It was quite a meaningful moment with nature that made me contemplate further the interconnectedness of life.

In addition to the regular program, we had the opportunity to participate in a sacred sweat lodge ceremony led by a local Native American healer. A sweat lodge is shaped much like an igloo, only it is made of sticks covered with blankets. Inside at the very center is a hole in the ground where hot rocks are placed. The ceremony involves sitting in a circle around the hot rocks while water is sprinkled over them to generate steam. The group is led in healing prayer to cleanse the body and mind, which opens the way to one's fundamental nature.

Afterward, as I was walking back to our yurt, I had an encounter with a chipmunk. He was standing on top of a stack of pine logs, chattering away with the other creatures in the woods. As I neared the woodpile, the chipmunk turned and faced me directly as if to acknowledge my presence. Then he continued to jabber on almost like he was trying to tell me something.

I watched in surprise as I remembered that a couple of months before, Desirée and I had attended another retreat where we took part in a process of guided imagery. In the exercise, we each partnered with someone and took turns symbolically retrieving for each other what early traditions might refer to as a "power animal." The idea was to get in touch with one's areas of disconnection with the Self. In this simulated rite of passage, each power animal that came forward would metaphorically reconnect you. My partner brought back to me a buffalo, a squirrel and a chipmunk.

So now, I felt compelled to pay attention to this chipmunk on the woodpile. The thoughts streaming through my mind were something like this:

Oh, don't you worry. This woodpile represents the stockpile of good fortune awaiting you. Continue stepping toward your dreams, and they will happen. Don't you worry about a thing....

After about two minutes, the chipmunk took one last look at me and then disappeared between two stacks of logs. Now I had to go beyond ordinary logic and accept what this unconventional moment had to give, even though some might think me silly to do so. It was a meaningful moment with nature that made me contemplate further the interconnectedness of life. Strangely, I felt a great deal of comfort.

Sneaky Pete, of course, went bonkers by saying, "Oh brother, now he's talking to a darn chipmunk."

Finally, I said back, "What's the matter with talking to a chipmunk? People talk to their dogs and cats much the same way. And besides, you know what, Sneaky Pete? The things you say to me are no more real than what the chipmunk said. Why should I listen to you any more than to him? Whenever I listen to you, I feel drained and disempowered. My encounter with the chipmunk made me feel good and optimistic."

At this point in my journey, my resistance began to wane. I was no longer troubled by the conversations or my unusual experiences. I began to understand that wisdom is the same no matter how it is delivered. I only needed the trust to follow my new direction.

This may be a good time to reflect upon a time in your own life when something occurred that seemed odd, yet natural. Did you dismiss it or contemplate the incident?

As you engage in the process of opening to new levels of awareness, you may begin having unusual experiences depicted in all spiritual traditions. The key is to keep yourself centered as you remember to stay in the present moment. You may also try slow, deliberate breathing or simply recalling your name.

At the end of the retreat, Desirée and I flew to Oakland and then drove home to Carmel. We were about 50 miles from our house when I received a new inner message regarding the apartments we owned in Oklahoma.

It is time to let the apartments go.

My first response was "No way." We had made this investment for a reason, and it was not part of our plan to sell them. Then a few minutes later, I got another message.

You need to use your gifts to help people.

As we came near the majestic Monterey Bay, I got yet another message.

You're done with this place. You'll be leaving soon. And yes, it is time to let the apartments go.

"Are you sure? That seems scary," I responded.

Yes, fear is what stops most people from achieving true wealth creation. You must keep going, and everything will work out fine.

"But what about my health?" I asked. "I'm not sure I am up to all this. And what about our money? How is that going to work?"

Don't worry about your health. You will become so fixed up that you won't even remember what you were like when you look back. Things will become clear in a few months. Just keep going, and all that you need will be given to you. First, you must learn to let go and trust. Only then can you see what is next. For now, you need to rest and surrender.

Buffalo Totem

We should take care not to make the intellect our God; it has,
of course, powerful muscles, but no personality.
—Albert Einstein, German-born physicist (1879-1955)

During the exercise where I had discovered my symbolic power animals, Desirée also discovered hers—a herd of rams, some wild horses, a cougar family and a herd of buffalo. Though our partners had each retrieved separate symbols, we were intrigued that the buffalo had come to us both. We learned that buffalo is about engaging in right prayer with right action, which in turn brings vast abundance.

We were, of course, elated with this news, as money concerns were at hand. I could get excited about right prayer with right action if it could actually solve my problems and lead to the abundance we were seeking. I just wasn't sure how to do this. But I could see how letting go would begin to remove our sense of struggle and allow the organizing principles of life to work in our favor.

▶ Buffalo Sign

Man has given up silent knowledge for the world of reason.
—Wayne Dyer, American author, *The Power of Intention* (1940-)

One morning a few weeks later, I woke up feeling particularly frustrated. By now, the idea of selling our apartments in Oklahoma City had thrown me over the edge. I did not want to let them go. We had worked hard to acquire our investment, and selling did not seem prudent. What's more, I was still vacillating with the whole notion of following the guidance anyway. Meanwhile, Wizard and Sneaky Pete were having some spirited discussions.

If at any point, you find yourself going through similar fluctuations— that is, feeling expanded, then confused or afraid—be assured that this is normal during times of transition. By now, I had become used to taking two steps forward and one step back.

Fortunately, Desirée was much more comfortable with guidance. She asked for a sign from the universe that would confirm we were on the right track in selling our apartments. "If this is what we are supposed to do," she requested, "I want a very clear sign, which to me would be something like our onsite apartment manager, Justin, quitting his job."

As it was, we had just talked with Justin the day before, and he showed no indication of quitting. In fact, he had expressed concern about losing his job due to downscaling within the primary management company. He wanted to stay with us because he liked his work. We had assured him that he would not lose his job due to us.

Two and a half hours later, the phone rang, and guess who it was? The voice on the other end said, "Oh hi, Desirée. This is Justin. I have some bad news. I just received a new job offer, and I'll be leaving Tudor Meadows in two weeks." We were both floored—and not because we were losing a valued manager.

Over the next few days, as we came to terms with what had taken place, I got angry with the higher power. I started shaking my finger at the sky and shouting, "Okay, I want my own sign. In fact, I want a big sign so there is no doubt about what we are doing and that selling our apartments is the right move. It was not our plan to sell our apartments at this time. It goes against everything we know about creating long-term financial wealth. What about maintaining assets to preserve cash-flow while building equity? And besides, our investment is doing quite well."

> You can ask for a sign from the universe to confirm that you are on the right track.

You may recall the scene in the movie *Forrest Gump* where Lt. Dan Taylor (the character who had lost his legs) was on the shrimp boat with Forest. He had climbed with his hands to the top of the mast and was bellowing his frustration at the heavens. I was having a similar moment, but I was shouting from my bed. "I want an unmistakable sign," I continued, "something like a live buffalo in downtown Carmel. Yes, that's it. You show me a buffalo downtown. And furthermore, make it clear that we can sell our buildings for 'x' dollars."

The amount I called out was higher than what I thought the market would actually bear, so neither of these signs was likely to happen. I felt pretty secure in my demands. I thought if the higher power could deliver these things, maybe I could get fully behind this guidance thing. And besides, I wanted Ol' Wizard to know how I felt.

You may be wondering about the idea of demanding a sign and getting angry at the higher power. This was just my own reaction to the frustration of being a slow learner. Your way of communicating may be different. Mostly, you just need to make your requests with sincerity and clear intention.

Later that morning, Desirée and I met with our friends Barry and Kipra in downtown Carmel during the famous Concours d'Elegance. Being at a car show and not a rodeo, we didn't seem to have much chance of seeing a live buffalo. Nonetheless, as the four of us wove our way along the rows of cars, I actually kind of kept my eye out for a buffalo. Now, I was *really* beginning to wonder about my sanity. Besides, I wasn't into cars much. I mostly went to enjoy Barry ogle over the exhibits.

There were no buffalo anywhere. I guess Sneaky Pete must have been right. This guidance stuff was just some airy-fairy, woo-woo nonsense for all those people who couldn't think for themselves. Yep, just like I suspected. The messages were probably my own thoughts or a bit of free-floating mind chatter. So there I had it—no buffalo, no guidance. Was I going off the deep end again?

You may want more wealth creation strategies at this point or find that my story does not fit entirely with your situation. The best strategy I have found is to utilize what forms the foundation of this book. That is, the Six Dimensions of Wealth Creation. Remember it is a reliable guide for finding your own way. It will point to the inherent wisdom within you as you focus on the dreams of your heart. Keep engaging the process until you have clarity about *your* true wealth direction and finding your purpose in life. I will also address more practical applications for wealth creation in the later chapters of the book.

▶ Write Books

The whole course of things goes to teach us faith. We need only obey. There is guidance for each of us, and by lowly listening, we shall hear the right word.
— Ralph Waldo Emerson American essayist and poet (1803-1882)

Over the next couple of weeks, I did not think about the buffalo. We were busy with a previously planned trip to Oklahoma City to check on our apartments and take care of business.

We flew into Dallas/Fort Worth, rented a car and first headed toward Austin to attend a workshop in Texas before going to Oklahoma City. The workshop was held at a beautiful new retreat center called The Crossings. Being there was revitalizing, and the tranquil retreat-campus inspired us. The ambience of the grounds struck a chord in me that seemed familiar, though this was my first visit. I could draw many parallels between The Crossings and the vision Desirée and I had for a retreat center, but again I wondered if I could live up to such a large undertaking.

One night, I was saturated with gentle whispers about writing books. The words reverberating in my mind were *Write books, write books, write books.* I ignored the messages at first, but they kept coming.

Finally I said back to the silent voice, "Write books?"

Yes, that is correct. Write books.

I didn't feel like adding anything new to my already overloaded psyche. I was busy relaxing, not looking to take on a new project. And besides, I had no idea what I would even write about. Later the next afternoon, I took a little nap only to hear the same words echoing stronger and louder:

Write books! Write books! Write books!

I questioned the voice again, "Write books?"

Yes, that is correct, Write books! Write books! Write books!

Now, keep in mind that I was about ready to put the whole guidance idea behind me and get on with my life, especially after not seeing my buffalo sign. But the voice was relentless. Finally, I responded, "Here we are trying to figure out whether to sell our apartments and move to Hawaii. You won't show me any buffalo, and now you want me to write books. And besides, I don't have time to write books." I decided to ignore the messages and not tell Desirée. But when I went to sleep that night, there it was again:

Write books, write books, write books.

And again,

Write books, write books, write books.

And then again,

Write books, write books, write books.

And then even more,

Write books, write books, write books, write books, write books, write books, write books, write books, write books, write books.

"Okay, I've had enough." This went all night—over and over and over. I could not make it stop. Finally I said, "What do you want me to write about?"

Well, you can write one book about living your soul's purpose, one about your loving relationship with Desirée, and maybe one about being with Fred. (Fred Jealous is a long-time mentor and friend of mine, as well as for many others)

Well…okay, I thought. I could get interested in doing this, maybe. But then I began thinking, how could I possibly write about living my soul's purpose? That was not how I had lived my life. And besides, I was having difficulty working at the computer. Yes, I enjoyed expressing myself through writing, but for several years being in front of the computer had made me tired and had an unpleasant effect on my nervous system. I used to think I was just sensitive to the electromagnetic fields, but putting my computer in another room and installing a liquid crystal display monitor did not seem to improve the problem. Over time, I determined that I was bothered by the flickering light, a sensitivity that seemed connected with the head fluttering I had experienced earlier in the year. The only effective way of dealing with it had been to limit my exposure.

So then I asked the Wizard, "What about the retreat center? I thought I was supposed to create a retreat center in Hawaii, and this would fulfill my soul's purpose? Frankly, I'm confused. And how do you expect me to trust any of this? And what about my buffalo sign?"

Don't worry about that. Clarity will come. Write books! Write books! Write books!

When I awoke early the next morning, I told Desirée about my conversation on writing books, at which point the Wizard backed off and let me rest.

▶ Buffalo City

The animal chooses the person, not the other way around.
—Ted Andrews, author of Animal Speak (1952-)

When Desirée and I left The Crossings, we drove to Oklahoma City as planned. Our first stop upon entering town was at the natural food store to pick up a few apples and snacks. We each liked to eat a Fuji apple every morning before breakfast. In the store, Desirée came across a pamphlet from some Kansas buffalo company promoting the health benefits of buffalo meat. I didn't know that buffalo meat has fewer calories, less fat and cholesterol, plus more iron and vitamin B-12 than chicken, pork, beef or salmon. I wondered if this could be my buffalo sign.

Sneaky Pete immediately jumped in with, "Yeah man, maybe you should eat some buffalo meat to help you manifest that incredible buffalo totem of abundance."

"Maybe you're right," I weakened. "It is just buffalo meat, and the only thing that resembles a live buffalo is the logo on the brochure. I'm sure Wizard can do better than that."

We left the store and drove toward the Westin Hotel in the heart of downtown. A few blocks before reaching our destination, I looked out the window. Standing at the edge of the downtown botanical gardens was a hand-painted, life-size statue of you'll never guess what.

I said to Desirée, "Hey honey, look at that buffalo statue."

"Oh, it's so pretty," she said. "I wonder if that is your sign."

"Nah. It's only a statue, not a live buffalo. It's probably been there awhile as part of the garden display."

We drove another block, and there on the corner stood another buffalo statue. It too was beautiful, hand-painted dark brown with a blue vest, a bright yellow scarf and a black cavalry hat. We turned the corner and saw two more buffalo statues. As we turned the corner again, we saw three more buffalo statues, one of which was smack in front of our hotel. Hmmm, this seemed really strange, I thought. Could all these buffalo be the sign I had asked for?

When we checked into our room, I looked out the window to see three more buffalo statues. One buffalo was painted white and gold with sequins to look like Elvis Presley. Another buffalo was painted like the American flag, and the third buffalo was bright purple. I stood there pondering.

Again shrugging off the buffalo signs to mere coincidence, we settled in by taking an afternoon nap. I mean after all, they were not live buffalo, and besides, the city was planning to put them there anyway. But I was beginning to wonder more seriously about so many buffalo. True, they were downtown, even if they were only statues. Maybe there was a slight possibility, even if only a remote one, that we were getting closer to a sign.

Sneaky Pete chimed in immediately, "Come on, man. Get real. You mean to tell me you're buying into this sign baloney? It's just a bunch of statues that were already there. No way were they intended to satisfy your ridiculous request for a sign. You're in Oklahoma, for Pete's sake."

"Yes, Mr. Pete," I replied, "Maybe we *are* in Oklahoma for your sake."

After we rested, Desirée went down to the fitness room for her workout, and I began clicking TV channels (one of life's simple pleasures). First I came upon a movie about a white guy living among a tribe of Native Americans. I clicked to the next station. After about ten rounds of surfing through the fifteen or so channels (I often don't stay on one more than a microsecond), I found myself fixated on a particular scene from the movie. For some reason, I was suddenly mesmerized. The white man and about thirty Native Americans were hunched down and stalking up a grassy hillside. Upon reaching the crest, they looked into a gorgeous valley to see herds and herds of buffalo. I mean thousands of them. The men got on their horses and moved in to take out a few buffalo for their tribe. If you've seen *Dances With Wolves*, you may recall the scene. But once again, I discounted the sign, telling myself that it was just a movie. I rolled over to take another nap.

Later that evening, Desirée and I walked toward Bricktown, an area of Oklahoma City where the streets have been bricked over. Running through the middle of Bricktown is a water canal flanked by quaint shops and restaurants. You can either walk on the sidewalks along the canal or take a water taxi to various locations. On the way, we came across more buffalo statues.

We stopped to dine at a place called Abuelo's before continuing our stroll along the canal. Again we encountered buffalo statues. One statue across from the ballpark was painted bright red. Another near the water taxi station was sky blue with clouds, and a black buffalo had been painted with white lines to look like a skeleton. Then we saw a brown buffalo, a gray buffalo, a buffalo on roller skates and one painted to resemble a Native American in full headdress. We must have seen more than forty buffalo statues scattered all over downtown! Could this indeed be my *downtown* buffalo sign? This was over the top.

We walked to the end of the canal and found a huge new store that had everything for the outdoors: gear for camping, boating, four-wheeling, fishing and gaming. We went inside only to find hanging right above the entry a stuffed buffalo head. This was a real one. Then we came across an entire family of real, life-size buffalo. Not only the head but the whole buffalo, body and all were right there in the center of the store. These were real animals, albeit stuffed, and there were three or four of them. As I marveled over the display, it seemed like one of them was staring me right in the eyes. I just stared back.

As we headed toward our hotel, I kept thinking this was some sort of enormous joke. I mean, what were the chances of this? I had asked for a sign, and now I couldn't seem to go anywhere without seeing buffalo.

The next morning, I awoke early. Eager to get outside, I went to see more buffalo statues. I took my camera and walked all over downtown taking pictures. I retraced the places we had been the night before and then ventured in the other direction to see if I could find more. I was completely enamored. There was a blue buffalo, and a silver one that looked like the buffalo nickel coin, and a splattered multicolor buffalo, and a buffalo statue wearing jewelry in front of a jewelry store and then a buffalo in a necktie. They were everywhere, beautiful and festive.

Desirée and I had an appointment to meet with one of our real estate advisors, so I finally had to stop. I had been out taking pictures for over an hour and a half. When I got back to the hotel, I realized that the Westin was sitting right smack in the center of them all. We were literally surrounded by buffalo statues during our four days in Oklahoma City. Since we had gone there to check on our apartments, I was beginning to connect the dots. But, Sneaky Pete was relentless in his mission to plant seeds of doubt. We had some serious debates along with the Wizard, who was just having fun.

If you would like to take a look at my photographs of the buffalo,
go to www.buffalototem.com

We left the buffalo behind as we drove to meet our advisor at Pearl's, a local restaurant located in the northwest part of town. We pulled into the parking lot, where we were once again greeted by a buffalo statue. This one was baby blue, and it was staring right at us. It was almost like the buffalo were following us around.

We visited with our advisor, who was very optimistic about our investment. Then after some casual chitchat and asking questions, we finally got around to what she thought was the value of our apartments. Her first words were, "If you're planning to sell, I'd list them for 'x' dollars." My jaw dropped open. I couldn't believe what I was hearing. The dollar amount she stated was the exact number I had shouted at the Wizard on the morning I was pointing and shaking my finger. I told her we would take that amount in a heartbeat. However, she went on to say that even though we should list them for that amount, we would likely get less. But we should get within 10 % of that number. I told her we needed to think about all this.

She asked us why we were thinking of selling. We told her that we were talking seriously about moving to Hawaii to create a retreat center. We didn't say anything about all the guidance stuff or the buffalo totem. We did not want her to think we had lost our marbles.

At that point, she asked if we would consider moving to Oklahoma City for a few years to become asset managers for some of her other clients who owned apartments. She was impressed by the way we had managed our 72 units, cleaning them up and improving the net operating income. We told her we were honored by her offer. A year ago we would have jumped at the chance, but now we were feeling pulled in another direction.

Inside, I felt torn. I knew this was going to make it even harder for us to let go of what we had established in Oklahoma City. We had the contacts, a great investment, a competent management company and we enjoyed going there to visit. We felt like stewards of the land and knew that our tenants were better off since we had owned the units. A real community feeling had developed between many of our tenants as a result of the changes we made.

Driving back to our hotel, we went a different way. The new entry point into downtown was highlighted with a quaint garden display and brick borders, beautifully landscaped with shrubs, smiling flowers and a vibrant leafy tree. Standing in front of the tree was another buffalo statue painted all over with Hawaiian flowers. Could this be our sign for Hawaii, we joked?

We knew we would have to let go of our apartments, and that this might be our last visit to Oklahoma City. But we were not quite ready to pull the trigger on selling. We spent the next couple of days grieving about letting go of our real estate direction. We had invested a lot of time and energy in this direction and in our new acquisition plans. However, we were now beginning to understand that this particular dream was not one that would fulfill our true wealth creation direction.

I think the hardest part was that we still didn't have a clear picture of how we would continue producing income once we let it all go. Sure, we'd have some cash from the sale of our investment, but we wanted to keep building wealth for the long term. During these moments, however, I began to understand that life was asking me to trust in my internal clarity more than in my fear about what would come next. I had wanted things to work the other way around. You know, show me the result first—then I will think about trusting.

▶ *Live Buffalo*

There are only two ways to live your life. One is as though nothing is a miracle. The other is as though everything is a miracle.
—Albert Einstein, German-born physicist (1879-1955)

Leaving Oklahoma City, we drove to Fort Worth, Texas for a visit with my nephew Cameron and his wife Denise, before returning home to Carmel.

On the way, we stopped for lunch at Chili's. After we ordered our food, I noticed a large painting of a buffalo with wings. The caption below said, "And Now They're Flying." This was apparently an advertisement for one of the specialty dishes, called buffalo wings. You'd think I'd had enough buffalo by this point. But I guess the Wizard wasn't finished with his cosmic fun and wanted to give me an unmistakable sign. I thought that if only I could see a live buffalo, then I'd have some real confirmation. Perhaps the Wizard thought showing it to me over and over would do the job and maybe keep my inner critic at bay for a while. One thing for sure, this experience was giving Sneaky Pete a run for his money.

At Cameron and Denise's house, the four of us were catching up on our lives when Denise said, "What would you like to do while you are here?"

I told her that I wanted to relax and visit, and that I'd like to see the Museum of Modern Art in downtown Fort Worth. I had heard that it was a pretty cool museum.

"Oh, that would be fun," she said. "And by the way, there is a beautiful nature preserve a couple of miles up the road from our house with some live buffalo. Would you like to go see them?"

I could not believe what I was hearing. "Yes, definitely," I said.

Now, we had visited Cameron and Denise twice before and neither of them had ever mentioned anything about the nature preserve or the buffalo. I was more than intrigued.

But then Sneaky Pete came on. "Okay, here are some live buffalo, but of course it's at a nature preserve, which is a likely place for buffalo to be found. Besides, this isn't exactly downtown Carmel."

"Oh, cram it," I said to Sneaky Pete. "Let's get on with seeing the buffalo."

The next morning on the way to the Museum of Modern Art, we all drove over to the nature preserve, which happened to be located on Buffalo Road (I'm not kidding). This was finally my opportunity to see live buffalo, but when we looked into the field where they normally graze, they weren't there.

"Come on now, Wizard," I called to my inner friend. "You're not going to put me through all of this and not show me the live ones are you? No live buffalo, no sign."

On the way home from the museum, we stopped by once more and again, no buffalo. We started getting back in the car to leave and looked up one last time. There herding out of the woods into the field toward us were six beautiful buffalo. There were my *live* buffalo at last.

▶ *One Last Totem*

All I have seen teaches me to trust the Creator for all I have not seen.
— Ralph Waldo Emerson American, essayist and poet (1803-1882)

The next day as Desirée and I headed back to Carmel, we drove toward the Dallas/Fort Worth Airport. Along the way we passed by a large water tower with a gigantic buffalo painted on the side of the tank. The inscription below read, "Buffalo Country." I thought, what a great sendoff, one last sign.

I'm sure you may be thinking that I was looking for buffalo at this point, but I really wasn't. I understand how once an object is in your conscious awareness, you begin to notice this same object everywhere. It's like when you are thinking about buying a particular new car; all of a sudden you notice that kind of car everywhere. Science will tell us that this one of the ways the mind works. What is referred to as our "reticular activation system" casts a net of attentiveness for whatever object has come into conscious awareness. Then the subconscious mind is unable to avoid noticing any such object within range of our peripheral vision. So it's almost like we have radar for a while for that particular object.

But something was more significant about these buffalo sightings. There were too many of them, and the timing connected my need for a sign with the experience. Synchronicity involves a phenomenon that is beyond ordinary coincidence. Carlos Castaneda used the term "cubic centimeter of chance" to describe that which exists beyond the normal bounds of reasoning. Through this experience of the buffalo, I was pulled further into the reality of guidance and our connection with life's essential unity. The synchronicity of it spoke to me on a deeper level than what I would chalk off as mere coincidence.

When you think about it, our whole world actually exists as an interconnected matrix of unseen relationships. Planet Earth sits within a galaxy of several billion stars called the Milky Way. The universe contains billions of galaxies. For Earth to sustain life requires multiple circumstances to fit within a very narrow range of parameters known in science as the laws of physics. Life requires numerous precise degrees of temperature, gravity and chemical compounds to remain within this range, or else all of life will perish. Much like the natural laws that sustain life, guidance is the inner technology that allows us to be consciously connected with the greater matrix. Guidance is what connects us with the clarity in our own system and our unique contribution to life.

During our flight home, I reflected upon all that had taken place, marveling at the buffalo. About the time we reached cruising altitude, I picked up a copy of Delta's *Sky Magazine* and began flipping through the pages. I rarely look at flight magazines, but for some reason I wanted to see this one. I opened it up to find a large photograph on a two-page spread. The image was a golden grassy field with a river running through it. I thought, what a wonderful place—Yellowstone. Then, once again the buffalo appeared. I was looking at a picture of a herd crossing the Little Firehole River in Montana.

I never did see a live buffalo anywhere downtown, but I think I had finally gotten the message. What do you think?

Take a look at your own life. Do you pay attention to the particular ways life communicates with you? What are the patterns or signs that keep recurring? You don't have to see a buffalo to find clarity, but you can ask for your own sign so that you will have confirmation for your true wealth direction. If life could speak directly to you, what would it say?

Tim's Story

Tim came to us when he was at a crossroads in his life. He had long worked in management for a pharmaceutical company. At the time, Tim was between jobs and was thinking about starting his own consulting company, but he had many limiting beliefs that were holding him back. He had difficulty trusting the inner signals he was getting. Using the guidance process, Desirée and I taught him how to validate his own inner clarity and apply it in his life. Discovering his purpose and true wealth direction was a major awakening for Tim. We helped him identify his inner conflicts and let go of the limiting beliefs that were stopping him from taking action. Within a few weeks, Tim had landed a major contract for his new business and went on to create enormous success.

Guidance

Points to Remember

- Allow yourself to open to your higher wisdom, even when you are afraid.

- Find language for your interior knowing that resonates with you, such as improved mental clarity, intuitive intelligence and so on.

- Take off the brakes and explore what calls to you. Let yourself imagine with the true wealth desires of your heart.

- Find experts in their fields in your areas of interest, ones who you can talk with to find out more about any new direction you may be considering. Work with a true wealth mentor who can help you learn to activate your deepest passions.

- Pay attention to your dreams when sleeping. What are they trying to reveal?

- The wisdom in your own system may come as intuitive hunches, gut feelings, just knowing, pictures, visions or words that appear. Don't edit what you get. Just listen.

- Keep a journal of the messages you receive. Use it for self-reflection, and look for repeating themes.

- Keep asking for clarity about your purpose in life and your true wealth direction until you get a response. Answers will come.

- Observe what may seem like coincidences as you look for new openings.

- Ask for inner guidance and clear direction as you step toward your true happiness goals while clearing your limiting beliefs and thoughts.

- If you're unsure about a direction, ask for a sign from the universe. Then let go, but pay attention.

For more powerful exercises about guidance that will help you achieve wealth from the inside out, download your supplementary *Wealth Creation Workbook* at www.WealthCreationWorkbook.com.

Chapter Five

RUMBLINGS

Juice Behind the Journey

The future belongs to those who believe in the beauty of their dreams.
— Eleanor Roosevelt , American First Lady and political leader (1884-1962)

I am going to break the chronology of my story to reveal some early rumblings that occurred before the ending of my construction activities. As I noted in Chapter Three, The Six Dimensions of Wealth Creation do not occur in any set order. For example, you'll recall that some people may have clear direction (sixth dimension) after an ending, (second dimension) and just need to work through their blocks (forth dimension). Others will instead want to focus on their rumblings (first dimension) to gain a deeper sense of their true wealth desires and repeating life themes.

Rumblings are the first steps of sensing your true wealth passions and finding your purpose in life, although you may not pay full attention to them until you have had an ending. You may experience rumblings as a discomfort that you can't quite explain, or as deep inner longings or yearnings. Rumblings are the intuitive whispers that call you. If you reflect upon your life, it is likely that rumblings have often prompted you toward your purpose. Look at the passions you pursued or wanted to pursue, the relationships that held special meaning and the ventures that called you to action. These are the rumblings that give you a sense of knowing or will lead you to knowing, if you are willing to pay attention. You may think of your rumblings as a kind of divine restlessness. They are an important foundation for discovering your purpose and creating Wealth Inside Out.

My journey along the six dimensions was peppered with rumblings for a long time before I was aware that I could tune into guidance, clear the past and choose to be in alignment with my purpose in life. I, like so many others, came to the path of purpose through discontent. As we explore the subject of rumblings, you may find that your personal experiences of reaching for true success and happiness will accumulate until they also hit a critical mass that finally finds expression.

> Look at the passions you pursued or wanted to pursue, the relationships that held special meaning and the ventures that called you to action.

Let's look at some of the rumblings I had before everything started falling apart. A series of events occurred that propelled me from one state of awareness to a completely different sense of reality, without any thought or action on my part. Or so it seemed.

My first rumblings came long before the buffalo, when I followed a boyhood dream to hike the Appalachian Trail, a 2100-mile footpath from Georgia to Maine. I also longed to meet and marry the woman of my dreams. Then there were a few false starts to be part of successful business ventures that would give me a sense of belonging. Through all these experiences, I had some awareness of what I came here to do. I just couldn't quite put my finger on it.

As you read the stories I'm about to share, you may reflect upon the rumblings from your own life. Do you have hints of what you most want to do? What is your sense about the special contribution you want to make? How long has this feeling been with you? In what ways have you attempted to fulfill these true wealth desires? Where did you give up and what were your successes?

A Boyhood Dream

To dream a dream,
The dream of all dreams,
Not as in a daydream
Or a dream you dream by night,
But a real dream,
A dream you go out and do—
It is here that the essence of life survives.

In 1984, when I was 28 years old, I wrote this poem, which reflects some of my early rumblings. This was the same year George Orwell had selected for the rumblings of society. Indeed, many of his prophesies about the great advances in civilization and technology have eventually come to pass. This was also the year that a special dream of my own came true.

My rumbling had begun 14 years before the poem was written when, as a young teenager, I found purpose in a wish to fulfill a certain dream. This happened in 1970 while I was on a weekend camping trip with three friends at Black Rock Mountain in Shenandoah National Park, Virginia, about 30 miles from where I had grown up.

The four of us settled into a trailside shelter, a three-sided lean-to designed for hikers and campers. We had in tow a few bottles of beer pilfered from the closet of one friend's dad, and thus began a leisurely walk through the woods. I didn't like beer, but I wanted to be cool, so I joined in as we walked and sipped. I made sure I was the last one in line. That way I could pretend to be drinking while I poured out my drink on the ground behind me.

It's funny how we come up with such ingenious ways of fooling others (and ourselves) in order to be a part of something or get what we want. I had done this in relation to finding my purpose for many years. Even at an early age, I felt connected with some greater contribution I hoped I would make to society one day. But our culture does not encourage us to explore such inner feelings, leaving us unsure, and our lives undeveloped.

Do you ever try to fool yourself or others? What ways do you attempt to fit in even when there is no fit? What approach would you like now for being encouraged toward your true wealth dreams?

The next day my friends and I hiked from the trail shelter to the top of Black Rock Mountain. The four of us had a blast bounding over huge boulders splattered with lichen, which gave us good traction for climbing. After a couple of hours, we slid back down to the trail. Leaning against warm rocks to rest, we absorbed magnificent views of the Shenandoah Valley with all its rich farmland.

As we sat there, two men with large backpacks stopped as well, and we chatted with them briefly. These guys looked like serious hikers on a trek of some sort.

"You mean this trail goes through 14 states all the way from Georgia to Maine? And you guys are walking 500 miles?" I marveled at what they had shared with us.

After a few minutes, the men continued on their way. I sat amazed at the idea of a 2100-mile footpath when suddenly, I felt a rumbling. Something in me knew that I too would hike this trail one day. I don't know how I knew, but I could feel it in my bones. In that moment, a dream was born in me. The four of us went back down to the shelter to eat lunch and "drink" some more beer, but I could not stop thinking about the Appalachian Trail.

Over the years, I often contemplated my dream to hike the trail. I wanted to set out on this adventure right after high school. Then when I graduated, I thought, well, maybe next year when I will be more ready. One by one, the years ticked by, and every year I had a new excuse. "Okay, next year when I have the money, or the one after that when I am more settled, or the next year when I find someone to go with me." Eventually, I forgot about my unfulfilled dream, but it never stopped nudging me.

> Was there ever a time when you just knew you would do something? What are some of the early rumblings you have had?"

Look now in your own life. Have you ever had an unfulfilled dream? Is the dream still alive? Are the reasons you gave for not fulfilling it still valid?

At the age of 27, I enrolled in a leadership training program. During the first weeks, we talked a lot about commitment and what we were up to with our lives. This got me thinking about my unfulfilled longings. One evening, I hosted an introductory meeting and was asked to share my experiences. I talked about the program and ended by saying, "You just have to do it. It is important to follow your dreams and do the things you most want to do."

As these words fell out of my mouth, enormous emotion welled up inside. Could this have been the early rumblings of my Wizard trying to awaken me? Looking back, I can clearly see that I was beginning to get in touch with my life's mission to help others realize their dreams. But first, I had to satisfy my inner rumblings. I had dipped into the pain of my unfulfilled dream to hike the Appalachian Trail, and I could no longer delay.

The next day, I called the program director and told her it was time to make my dream come true. Six weeks later at the summit of Springer Mountain, Georgia, I finally began my personal walk in the woods. I still didn't have the money or the time or the right person to hike with, but I was hiking. I was doing it. Finally, I had stepped forward without waiting for every circumstance to be just right.

I had wonderful experiences during my 6-month excursion. The outer journey of walking in nature taught me about the inner journey of perseverance. I encountered the hardship and loneliness of life on the trail, as well as the ecstasy of its simplicity. The harshness of nature's elements were balanced with her breathtaking beauty. I think one of my favorite things was meeting such interesting people in a sort of traveling community of hikers that emerged along the way. Quite often several of us would walk together for the day or meet up at mealtimes. At night around the fire, we told jokes and stories and sang songs.

On September 12, 1984, I stood atop of Mt. Katahdin in Baxter State Park, Maine. I had triumphed. Having followed the rumblings from my teenage adventure, I had at last fulfilled my dream. I did not make any money while hiking the trail, but through this experience I had achieved a type of physical, interpersonal and spiritual wealth. I could now go on to what was next. The Appalachian Trail experience soon became a metaphor for everything else I would do. I had felt a sense of purpose, the completion of which was an important milestone toward something bigger.

The early rumblings I had about hiking the Appalachian Trail were similar to the ones I would later have about meeting Desirée and about writing books. This was the same kind of inner knowing I was to have about finding my place in the field of success coaching and wealth creation trainings.

Look into your own life. What are some of the early rumblings you have had? Was there ever a time when you just knew you would do something? What is the *someday* you are dreaming about now?

Entrepreneurial Ventures

It is a mistake to suppose that men succeed through success;
they much oftener succeed through failures.
—Samuel Smiles, Scottish author and reformer (1816-1904)

In the early 1990s, I began having rumblings to create a business with shared leadership and the camaraderie of a business partnership, something that also served a broader market than my construction business. I wanted a perpetual type of commerce that did not require starting anew with every project, as did the building industry. I wanted to have a more substantial impact in the world.

I moved from Monterey to San Diego in 1994 to begin a new greeting card company called Ideal Visions. There I teamed up with two others to develop a vision after John Lennon's song "Imagine." However, we were never able to measure up to the message of this song. The three of us started off with different styles from the beginning and never could align them. Somehow the business still managed to go far, even with the disharmony. We created a line of beautiful handmade cards, and my rumblings about purpose trickled into the card's messages along with a theme of honoring the world's many traditions. We manufactured at a *maquiladora* (Mexican factory) in Tijuana and distributed in the United States to specialty boutiques. My job was to build the systems for the business and oversee production.

By the time I left the company, we had nearly 100 products and more than 600 customers. In brief, after two years of learning much about business and about manufacturing in Mexico, I ended up penniless. My time at the *maquiladora* was the most rewarding part of the enterprise. I cultivated a bond with the Mexican people who made our products. I didn't speak Spanish, nor they English, but somehow we communicated and had a strong connection. The production atmosphere was energizing, but I could not create this same dynamic with my partners. The pressure of our insufficient startup resources and our inexperience pulled us toward discord, which eventually eroded our desire to work together.

In hindsight, I could see the signs of strain in this venture from early on. I learned that relationships often continue the way they begin and that sharing similar values is important. We were not clear about the business vision and each other's expectations. My desire for this entrepreneurial triumph had not been realized, but I had learned an important lesson.

How does this look in your life? Have you ever been involved in a project where the relationships were strained, even though you may have been energized by the endeavor? How did this experience contribute to what you are currently doing or the relationships you have now?

After the Ideal Visions adventure, I took several months getting in touch with where to focus next. I could again feel the rumblings of my lifelong passion for the personal development field.

Though I did not connect with the idea of purpose at that time, my focus began to shift from how to make a living to what was calling me. Have you ever asked the question "What would I like to do even if I didn't have to work?"

In 1996, I created a dynamic curriculum called Committed Listening, followed by an outgrowth program, called Total Relationship Success. I felt closer to my true wealth niche with this work, but my understanding about the seminar business was limited. I began teaching classes and worked privately with individuals. People enjoyed working with me as well as the results they attained, and I was doing what I loved. Yet looming debts remained from my previous business, and I had no clue how to market myself to obtain results fast enough to make a living. I continued these programs for a couple of years before taking another detour.

> It is one thing to understand concepts and another to live authentically with what you have learned.

It was only a matter of time, however, before I would eventually understand how to make it happen. I had been in touch with this vision ever since I was 25 years old when I was walking with a friend, talking about how I would one day be leading retreat programs. This was before I had any experience with retreats or the process of how to become successful. My rumblings for creating retreats have been inside of me as if they are a part of my being. What are the rumblings inside of you that keep coming back?

Meeting Desirée

Always bear in mind that your own resolution to succeed is more important than any other.
—Abraham Lincoln, 16th American President (1809-1865)

One of my deepest desires was to meet and marry the woman of my dreams. Then with wonderful timing, Desirée came into my life. I concluded that if I was this broke and she wanted me anyway, then her love must be genuine. I began a powerful time of connecting in many ways with my life mate. I had recently contemplated why I was still single and so began to focus on finding my life partner. When I was young, I thought I would marry in my late 20s, but my 20s came and went. Soon my 30s were nearly gone, a shocking realization. I decided to make finding a partner a priority and set out to learn everything I could about healthy, loving, committed relationships.

Remember, the true desires you have for any positive purpose are themselves the rumblings that lead you toward fulfillment. Rumblings are one of the ways your soul speaks to you. Whenever you satisfy a rumbling, you are, by nature, achieving Wealth Inside Out in some aspect of your life. You'll see from the story that, essentially, I went through all Six Dimensions of Wealth Creation on my journey to meeting Desirée. Those of you currently looking to find your life partner may want to take special notice as I share a few of the tips I learned for relationship success.

I came upon a class for men called How to Meet and Marry the Woman of Your Dreams, which piqued my interest, especially since it was taught by a woman. I went to the class to find an attractive teacher in a room of 50 men. Maureen had a comforting manner, and her class was about how a man might approach a woman in an ordinary place, such as the grocery store or post office, so that he would likely get a favorable response.

Your first words might be about something general, such as the weather, followed by something like, "Is this where you normally shop?" or "The sweater you're wearing is a great color for you." The idea is to gently move into a conversation. Even if the woman is not immediately responsive, if she continues standing there, she's interested. You might have to carry on the conversation alone at first, but keep it light and funny if you can. After a few minutes of conversation, you may say that you'd enjoy talking with her further and then ask her to meet you at the coffee shop close by. The idea here is to give her an opportunity to feel more comfortable with you in public. There in a coffee shop, she hasn't yet given you her phone number or other personal information, so it is a safe, neutral place.

Next, Maureen taught us a bolder approach. Simply tell the woman that you find her attractive and would like to talk with her. Maureen and her assistant would role-play these approaches with different men in the class, then critique each man's effectiveness. The exercise spoke to me because I often felt intimidated when approaching single women. Half the problem of connecting involves nothing more that having the courage to talk to someone you find interesting. This same principle applies to any endeavor. Do you have the courage to step toward the kind of wealth you want?

A few days later, I called Maureen for a private consultation over the phone. I told her that I kept finding women who were either unavailable or who didn't treat me well. She then guided me through some powerful exercises that helped me understand how I was getting in my own way. One insightful comment she made was, "Mark, do you realize that the woman you are looking for is also looking for you?" Never before had it occurred to me that somebody would actually be out there looking for me. That realization totally changed my perspective, freeing me up on many levels. You can see how harnessing the experience of experts, will help you succeed more rapidly.

I picked up some enlightening books about the characteristics of healthy relationships and lasting love. This helped me deal with the other half of my problem, being attracted to women who were not suitable for me. I had the bad habit of seeking out the unavailable, the unlikely or the troubled—what one author termed "relationsickness." I had much work to do around the subject of intimacy.

Finally, I had to shift my focus to the question of what I wanted in a relationship. I asked myself, "How do I want to *feel* when I am with someone? What do I feel after I've been with her? Is she interested in me as much as I am in her?" I learned how to *be* a good partner for someone else and how to create more relationship success possibilities.

Many changes occurred inside of me over the next months, but the real test would be what was actually happening in my relationships. It is one thing to understand concepts and another to implement what you have learned. It did seem like the work I had done with my relationship success mentor and the books I had read were clearing old patterns so I could eventually find my life mate and spiritual partner.

I began to get past being nervous about approaching women, but I kept making some of the same mistakes by getting involved with the wrong women. As I observed my own behavior, I eventually came to understand that I was terrified of commitment and that was the underlying cause of why I attracted unfulfilling relationships. I realized later that this exasperating pattern had shielded me from facing my own fear. I guess it is always easier to point the finger at others instead of dealing with one's own unresolved issues. One-by-one, I put an end to these ineffective patterns. Although I had some ups and downs, I was learning from my mistakes.

You may find rumblings from your own life where fulfillment seems slow in coming. You may ask yourself: How important is the success and happiness I want? Am I entirely willing to do what it takes to fulfill my true wealth rumblings? Will I make these my priority? Have you considered finding an expert mentor or expanding your knowledge and skills in the area of life you want to fulfill? We will address the importance of specialized education and training in greater detail in Chapter Six.

One day in June of 1997, I was in the Encinitas area of San Diego taking a rest near the beach. A friend who was teaching a day-long seminar nearby had invited me to come to her class and talk about my Committed Listening program. So I headed over to the seminar. On my way, I had an unusual premonition as I pondered the words, *You're going to meet your girlfriend.* I immediately thought to myself, "Okay, I'm ready for that." Could these rumblings have been more early messages from the Wizard?

When I entered the classroom, I was instantly drawn to a beautiful, petite woman sitting on the sofa. Our eyes met when right away she looked back at me. I thought to myself, "This must be the woman I'm supposed to meet."

When the class ended and my teacher-friend introduced me to the group, I talked about my program and handed out brochures. Afterward while people were dispersing, I went over to talk with the beautiful woman, Desirée. She seemed warm and friendly, and I was mesmerized by her presence. A few minutes later, I went outside trying to muster the courage to speak with her alone. As she was getting into her car, I blurted out, "I'm really attracted to you. Are you single?" I was nervous and fumbling, but I didn't care. I knew I had to see her again.

Desirée looked up at me with her clear blue eyes and said, "Well, I'm separated from my husband, but we're trying to work it out."

My heart sank. I thought, well here I go again finding someone who is not available. What came out of my mouth next took me by surprise.

Like a total klutz, I said something like, "Oh gee, let me know if it doesn't work out." In my attempt to recover I said, "Well, why don't you come to my weekly class. Oh, don't worry about what I just said. I will be respectful of where you are with your situation. So if you are drawn to my program, don't let my comments deter you."

She drove off, and I went to a party where I ran into Kamilla, another friend, whom I told about meeting Desirée. I still felt embarrassed about what I had said to her, having always viewed marriage as a sacred bond. Really, I did not want to be in the middle of someone else's relationship problem.

Kamilla replied, "Oh, don't worry about it. She was probably very flattered," which helped me relax.

A couple of hours later, I called home to check my voice mail and heard a soothing voice… "Hi Mark, this is Desirée; you know the one you met earlier today. What I want to say is this." Now it seemed that she was the one who was nervous. "I'm interested in a friendship. I want to make it clear that I'm not available for dating, but you seem like someone I'd like to know. Our friendship would have to be strictly platonic, so if you are interested, please call me."

The next day I returned Desirée's call, and we talked for nearly three hours. A week later, she came over, which began a wonderful new friendship. Desirée did enroll in my class and often arrived early so we could visit. We usually went out for a bite to eat, sharing with each other the latest in our lives.

While I had continued dating other women during this time, I never really made a connection. Seven months later, Desirée decided to finalize her divorce. Now something new began to emerge between us. As time went on, the energy between us grew more electric, and my rumblings for this kind of connection were finally being fulfilled. Desirée and I were off to a whole new life together.

Now let's look at my relationship story through the Six Dimensions of Wealth Creation. First were my rumblings; I identified my desire to find my life mate. Then there were endings as I let go of old ways. I turned to inner guidance as I began sensing my way toward new resources. I came upon a journey through the void as my capacity for relationship harmony eventually reorganized at a new level. To clear my way, I took classes, read books and hired expert mentors. Can you see how I was able to eliminate my limiting beliefs about relationships as I gained new knowledge and fresh perspectives? When going through this, I continued making my dream of finding my life mate a priority, while paying attention to what was choosing me. My purpose was fulfilled when Desirée and I eventually got together. Notice how I had remained clear about what I wanted even during our time of friendship. I was not *waiting* for Desirée. In time, she simply found new clarity for herself, and together we decided to join our lives.

Take a moment to look at what areas you might wish to change. Are you willing to make your dreams a priority as you travel the Six Dimensions of Wealth Creation? What are the true wealth rumblings speaking to you now, and what kinds of training might you need to begin stepping forward?

Getting Money Handled

Your net worth to the world is usually determined by what remains after your bad habits are subtracted from your good ones.
—Benjamin Franklin, American scientist, politician and writer (1706-1790)

Fast forward to the fall of 1998, when Desirée and I left San Diego to look for our personal paradise—a small community with warm weather. We talked about Hawaii, but we were not ready to make that kind of move. So we explored a few areas along the California Coast from Laguna Beach to Sebastopol. Before meeting Desirée, I had lived on the Carmel-Monterey Peninsula for 17 years and had many connections there. Although Carmel did not offer the climate we were seeking, we decided that this was our best choice.

After the two undercapitalized business ventures of the last four years, and being over $70,000 upside down, I was thinking about my rumblings for financial stability. To get the ball rolling, I went back into construction, a business I already knew how to market. Desirée and I also began talking about getting money handled for the long term. The question was how? I was so broke, I could barely see how I would meet my monthly expenditures, much less creating wealth.

Sneaky Pete chimed in as usual. "I don't like this idea very much, Mark. Everybody knows the simple formula: You have to work hard for money. Why do you want to waste your time chasing financial pipe dreams? Why don't you get a good job and be happy? Everybody knows that money is scarce and hard to get."

Even with Sneaky Pete's attempts to chase away my dreams, I knew I needed to create a set-up where never again would I be in such an economic position. We set out to learn everything we could about wealth creation.

▶ Commodity Futures

Even though you may not be good at everything, take time developing what you need to learn and your world will change rapidly.
— Robert Kiyosaki, American businessman and author (1947-)

We started out by ordering a home study course on commodity and options trading. We read the material, listened to the tapes, opened our trading accounts and off we went. Our first trades were in corn, cattle and sugar. Every morning at 6:00 o'clock, we would wake up and run to look at the computer screen to see if we were making money. After a few weeks of trading, we went long on gold. Then a few days later, gold went limit up—the maximum limit allowed on any particular day. The limits are set by the Securities and Exchange Commission (SEC) to regulate commodities from getting too far out of balance from the real market. Anyway, gold went up for several days in a row, and we sold. This was exciting. We had turned $350 into more than $4,000. Surely we could get rich doing this.

Everyday we studied our charts and made some more trades, but we quickly learned that not all trades went as smoothly as the gold had gone. Within a few weeks, we were back down to about half of our gains. Our emotional ups and downs moved right along with the markets, and this began to wear on our peace of mind. One of the first lessons we learned was that good traders aren't emotional about it. If you were to talk to one on the street, you wouldn't be able to tell whether the person was having a good or a bad day. We began to realize that neither of us had the emotional makeup of a model trader. Desirée especially rode this roller coaster of feelings. As the commodity values went up, she would get all excited and jump for joy, and as they went down, she would slide into anxiety and worry. I was perhaps a little more contained, but not much.

One of the programs that Desirée and I now teach is to help stock traders determine their unique personality style for making money. If the wealth creation program you are trying to implement (even if you are using a good one) is not the right fit for your personality, you will always be swimming upstream. Why not find the right wealth creation direction that already is a natural fit for your unique way of achieving success?

We switched from commodity futures to commodity options, because you can leverage your upside potential with less risk. We read several books on trading, from the technical aspects to the psychology. The books all agreed that the primary factor that determines success is your internal mindset. We had made up our minds and set our intention, thinking we would eventually get good at it. But if your mindset is not in the right place, you may actually read the trading charts incorrectly. That is, you will read information into a chart that is not actually there, or you will miss what it is telling you altogether. Sometimes when I would review a trade, I was utterly mystified at how, in retrospect, the charts could look so different than what I had seen at the time of the trade. This insightful lesson reinforced the importance of being in the right mental and emotional state for whatever one is doing. And being well-matched for how you make money is crucial. To make money, it is always best to do what you love to do, and you must also make sure that what you do for money fits your unique personality style, which can now be measured scientifically.

During our path to Wealth Inside Out, Desirée and I discovered a powerful instrument that measures your unique style of wealth creation. You will learn to recognize the natural motivators that compel you into effective action. The assessments also help you see yourself the way other people see you, which gives you a tremendous advantage when communicating your wealth vision with others. The personality and behavioral styles methodology is beyond the scope of this book, but you can find out more about these powerful instruments at our Website at www.WealthInsideOut.com.

Over the next year, we learned several trading strategies, but we both tired of looking at the computer to play a game we didn't find energizing. We had fun when we were making money, but this way of wealth creation did not fit our personality styles. Desirée is very much a people person, and I enjoy a variety of tasks that produce more tangible outcomes for other people.

By the time we were about $12,000 ahead, we slowly phased out of our remaining trades, eventually concluding that this way of life was not for us.

Sometimes it is important to try new things, if for no other reason than to find out what you don't want. However, when you tap into what you truly want, that is when you will be able to create wealth and happiness. Whenever you embark upon a new direction, ask yourself, "Is this really the wealth creation game I want to play?" Then listen.

▶ Building Again

One secret of success in life is for a man [or woman]
to be ready for his opportunity when it comes.
—Benjamin Disraeli, British statesman (1804-1881)

During our brief careers in trading, our construction business was starting to take off. I thought I had left construction forever when I moved to San Diego, but my rumblings for camaraderie and shared leadership were now being met with a new business partner in the industry.

This turned out to be an exciting time in my construction career. We were building an unusual house on the Big Sur Coast. Every wall and roofline was either curved or angled. Several months into the project, we

> One of the sales secrets I had learned was to go to the top of the ladder first. Then everyone you meet is suddenly receptive.

began to grow our company through a marketing outreach to various developments in the area. One development in particular encompassed a large tract of land with the kinds of houses we wanted to build.

I called the developer, and we met with him a few days later. We asked about his vision and shared ours with him. During the conversation, he made some comments that altered the course of our company. "You don't know any masons, do you? I'm having difficulty getting what I need," he said. Then he joked, "I'm about ready to fly to another country and bring some masons back."

At the time, nothing stood out about these comments, but over the next few days I couldn't stop thinking about them. As we rode back to our car with a couple of employees from the development, I had a feeling that we would be providing a valuable service there.

So I said, "It's nice to meet you. We'll be seeing more of you soon."

It was like the future we were about to have with them was already present. I have experienced this mysterious feeling a number of times in my life. Could this have been my Wizard lurking about again?

Take a look in your own life. Was there ever a time when you had a sense about something happening and subsequently it did?

A couple of days later, I said to my partner, "You know, that guy is looking for a solution to his masonry problem, and I think we can solve it."

"Nah, I don't want to do that," he said. "Let's just focus on building houses."

I dropped the subject, but a few days later I picked it up again. I wasn't focused so much on *how* we could solve the masonry dilemma. I just knew we could. In a couple of weeks, I again approached my partner, "We just have to pursue this masonry idea. Let's look at the resources we already have. What about the guy who works on your ranch who is from a village in Mexico where there are a lot of masons? He knows some of them who are here in the United States with legal papers. With our ability to organize and your connections, there's no reason why we can't put together a team of skilled masons. They would benefit from having well-paying jobs, and we would be at the top of the ladder with the managing partner. It's likely we would have all the work we wanted for the next 20 years. At least it's worth a shot."

Take notice of how, when you have clarity, there is a desire to take action even when others may not agree. When in your life did you have a natural momentum for a particular endeavor? This is the kind of thrust—the wisdom within your own system—that propels you forward regardless of obstacles.

A few days later, I called the developer again and made a proposal, "I think we can solve your masonry problem." I explained that although we weren't a masonry company per se, we had the ability to organize the necessary skill around his specific objectives.

He invited us out again, only this time he introduced us to his construction manager, who was at first a bit reserved. One of the sales secrets I had learned was to go to the top of the ladder first, which in this case, was the developer. Then everyone you meet is suddenly very receptive. This is exactly what happened, and within a few weeks we had a contract with a substantial advance for a multimillion dollar venture. We hired more than 30 masons and went to work on all the projects in the development requiring stonework.

What an expansive time this was. We were off and running with unstoppable momentum. We had the beginnings of a successful venture that held vast potential, and I was finally on the way to fulfill my rumblings for this kind of enterprise.

▶ *What's My Lesson?*

> You cannot create wealth by blaming others. You must begin to take responsibility for your own circumstances.

While handling all of our responsibilities for the project, we had also invested in our company infrastructure. We wanted to make sure we could easily accommodate any future requirements. However, there was one problem that I had not foreseen. A few months into the project, my business partner began moving away from the relationship and toward his own direction. It was clear that he wanted full ownership of the new masonry company. After some unruly disagreements on how to solve the matter, I decided to sell my portion, yet I went on to complete the residential project down the Big Sur Coast.

For a long time, I was disturbed by what had taken place. In situations like these, it is tempting to point the finger of blame at the other person. But you cannot create wealth or relationship success by blaming others. You must begin to take responsibility for your own circumstances. I became more curious about why I had attracted circumstances that were nearly identical to my previous business ending. I wanted to make sure I did not repeat this scenario yet again.

I spent a lot of time healing my self-confidence and clearing any programming that would attract more unwanted situations. I took a fresh look at my own shortcomings and again realized the importance of choosing people already aligned with a common vision.

All of us have themes that tend to keep repeating in our lives until we learn what life is trying to teach us. Identifying the mental environment to which we are exposing ourselves is important in transforming these themes. From there, we can interrupt the pattern as we move more fluidly toward what we most desire.

My recurring themes revolved around relationships and jobs that I no longer wanted to do. Going back to construction over and over was a part of my plight. It was the only reliable way I knew to make money. But now, my desires for doing what I truly loved were kicking into gear.

My lessons would require me to start down a new path even amid fear and unpleasant circumstances, and before I was ready. I would need to gain fresh knowledge, find new mentors and eventually come to a new level of clarity—one that I had never known.

What are the unwanted themes in your life that seem to keep recurring? Is there something you want to change but don't know how or where to begin? Becoming aware of your recurring patterns and what you want to change is the first step to clearing, which we will address more fully in Chapter Six.

▶ Real Estate Riches

Luck is a matter of preparation meeting opportunity.
—Oprah Winfrey, American talk show host (1954-)

As the Big Sur project neared completion, I was ready for another break from building. Desirée and I attended numerous seminars on real estate investing and various entrepreneurial ventures. You name it, and we probably did it. This was quite an expansive time as we traveled to many places around the United States and made discoveries seldom revealed in traditional learning venues. Something about the seminar environment stirred me. It was more than motivational; I felt at home, and I loved learning and watching others in their "aha!" moments.

Sneaky Pete was again trying to intervene. "Why in the heck are you wasting your time and money on these expensive seminars?" he kept saying. "Can't you see they aren't taking you anywhere? Why don't you just keep doing construction? It's the only way you've ever made money. Besides, you're good at it. Why not settle down and enjoy what you have?" But Sneaky Pete's attempts to squash my enthusiasm were not enough to quiet my rumblings.

Notice how every time I had thoughts about my true wealth desires my negative voices came on even stronger. What thoughts do you have that trigger your critical voices? How do you talk to yourself about the life goals you most desire?

As Desirée and I kept looking to find the right business, we came across many wonderful teachers. We met enterprising entrepreneurs and compelling speakers. We were encouraged by the story of one man who started with nothing and found success through real estate investing. Another taught us about the seminar business, which stirred my rumblings to look at where I might fit into the speaking industry.

Another teacher was Robert Kiyosaki (1997/1998), author of *Rich Dad, Poor Dad*. The subtitle, *What the Rich Teach Their Kids About Money That the Poor and Middle Class Do Not*, really captured my attention. Kiyosaki does an excellent job explaining how the system of money works in the real world. Regardless of how much you like or don't like the system, understanding how it actually works and working with it (or not) will determine your level of financial independence.

Desirée and I were riveted with this education and we learned new ways to think about money. We began to understand the inner dynamics of successful entrepreneurs as we learned about the power of systems, teams and leverage. One point in particular that hit home was to understand the difference between selling our time for money and setting up business structures that produce cash flow. Now all we needed was to apply these principles to our situation.

We chose apartments as our primary real estate focus and set out to learn everything we could. We looked at over 300 real estate proformas and personally visited more than 100 properties. We looked in California, Texas, Idaho, Arizona, Tennessee and Oklahoma. Finally, we hooked up with a company that does market research on apartment sectors, and this got us comfortable to buy our first property.

At one point, we became discouraged, thinking that we didn't have the knack. Then we learned about a powerful clearing process designed to eliminate the blocks that have prevented one from achieving the highest levels of success. We also discovered a wonderful retreat program held in Texas that offered a variety of life skills and success-development courses.

Prior to this, we had booked a flight into Dallas, Texas, from where we could drive to Oklahoma City to look at investment property. It turned out that we could also attend some courses at the retreat. The timing worked out perfectly, and we spent about a week in Texas learning new skills. Interestingly, Robert and Kim Kiyosaki showed up while we were there, which gave us the opportunity to hang out with the two of them and one other couple for 5 days. By the time we left our retreat, we had signed a contract to purchase the 72 apartment units in Oklahoma City (the same ones I mentioned earlier).

Our plan was to refinance them in a year or two, using that money to buy more units until we would fulfill our dream of financial independence. The only flaw in our plan was that we still needed to have a primary income while putting everything together. We looked at many businesses, from retail and franchises to day spas and automotive repair. Next we took a turn learning how to buy and sell foreclosure properties, but this only took us further off track. Desirée shares that story in Chapter Nine. We were still focused on doing what we *had* to do so we could do what we *wanted* to do. We had not yet tapped into what was truly calling us.

Looking back, I could see that even before we took any steps toward financial freedom, I had been restless. It was clear that each experience along the way was pointing me toward my true wealth purpose. Although Desirée and I had reached great success in the first steps of our plan, life was now taking us in a new direction.

What steps did you take in your life that ultimately led to something different? Can you see that your rumblings are what lead you into experiences that later point to how you will work in the world?

R-Group

Friends...they cherish one another's hopes.
They are kind to one another's dreams.
—Henry David Thoreau, American author (1817-1862)

While Desirée and I were focused on our elusive search for the right business opportunity, we had paid the price of a limited social life.

New rumblings for deeper social connections now began pulling at us. We were delighted when mutual friends introduced us to Barry and Kipra, who had recently moved from San Diego to Carmel. I introduced them to David, a long-time friend

> Through our successes and failures along the way, we build the inner strength for what will ultimately bring us true wealth and happiness.

and architect, as they were considering renovations on their house. Barry and Kipra invited David and his mate, Annee, and Desirée and me for dinner. The six of us had a remarkable rapport. We laughed a lot as we shared about our lives.

From this experience, R-Group (short for Our Group) was born, and we continued get-togethers two or three times per month. We took turns hosting meetings and cooking for the group. Sometimes we picked a topic to discuss or followed a preplanned format, but mostly we talked about what was going on in our lives. We also encouraged one another with our respective dreams and goals.

That year and a half with the six of us was filled with memorable experiences, and it provided valuable support not always easy to find. It is interesting that R-Group had come together without anyone making it happen. Desirée and I had set our intention for a connection like this, and in time, our rumblings emerged in their own natural way.

One evening I read aloud to R-Group some of my journal messages from the Wizard, thinking surely they would confirm that I was losing my marbles. Instead, the response was exactly the opposite. They seemed excited for me and encouraged me to continue. Each time we met over the next couple of months, I would read new messages and be surprised at how much they enjoyed them.

About the time that R-Group began, I decided it was time to find my true wealth niche in life. This was when I gathered the books, pamphlets and magazines related to personal growth and success development that I discussed in Chapter Two. The collage I created and showed everyone in R- Group was a visual symbol and a declaration of where I belonged in life. Although I did not know the exact details, it felt good to say aloud, "I belong in there somewhere."

I would soon learn about my Wizard and a new kind of logic—the secure inner reference place that begins from within one's heart. And this brings us full circle to where my story began.

You can see that all of a person's experiences are part of life's inherent design. As human beings, we are natural wealth creators, always looking to express and fulfill our rumblings. Life is forever leading all of us toward the realization of our purpose in life and Wealth Inside Out. The choice is whether or not to follow the desires of heart and soul. Through our successes and failures along the way, we build the inner strength for what will ultimately bring us true wealth and happiness.

Jenna's Story

Jenna came to me and wanted to meet and marry the man of her dreams. She had dated a number of men and had been in several long-term relationships. Similar to the way I had done with women prior to overcoming my relationship problem, Jenna kept meeting the wrong kinds of men. I helped her identify her rumblings for a loving, committed partner and then we mocked up a powerful relationship vision of her ideal mate. Using the powerful belief clearing techniques from our one-on-one wealth mentoring courses, I helped Jenna remove her unwanted negative beliefs about having healthy relationships with men.

A few months later, Jenna began seeing one of her coworkers, which began her first experience of the kind of connection she had always wanted. She later reported to me the following: "Working with Mark I learned to recognize what I had tolerated for so long. Now my whole life revolves around people who support me." Not long after that, Jenna married the man of her dreams and now has two beautiful children.

Rumblings

Points to Remember

- Rumblings are not generated through ordinary logic; become aware of what you feel internally. What is your true wealth vision?

- Begin to sense any discomfort that you can't quite explain, as well as the deep inner desires that signal your rumblings.

- Think of your deepest yearnings to feel congruent with the various aspects of your life. What is truly calling you?

- Don't wait for the right circumstances to be present; your rumblings will continue nudging you until you find a way to fulfill them.

- Do not let past failures prevent you from beginning again. Whenever you start anew, it is always with greater wisdom than before.

- Acquire new education. It might not necessarily be in a school, but learn about subjects that interest you. Read, attend workshops, listen to home study courses, join support groups, find an expert mentor or coach who can help you follow your dreams.

- Pay attention to what life is trying to teach you through your experiences and circumstances. What are your lessons?

- Make a collage that represents where you belong in life. Then look at it every day until your true wealth vision becomes clear.

- Rumblings are an important foundation for finding your purpose in life and creating Wealth Inside Out.

For more powerful exercises about rumblings that will help you achieve wealth from the inside out, download your supplementary *Wealth Creation Workbook* at www.WealthCreationWorkbook.com.

Most people never run far enough on the first wind to find out if they've got a second.
—William James, American philosopher (1842-1910)

Chapter Six

4th
Dimension

CLEARING

A Personal and Spiritual Makeover

We don't see things as they are, we see them as we are.
— Anais Nin, French-born author (1903-1977)

After a dose of life's endings and rumblings, what a relief it is to turn to guidance and higher purpose. But we still may need to recalibrate our mind and body to accommodate new perspectives, which requires a new capacity in perception. Intellectually we may know there is more to life, but emotionally we do not buy in. Although perspectives can shift in an instant, it can take a while to reorient our lives, even when we cooperate with the process.

Desirée and I had "downloaded" a powerful vision through expanded realms of perception, yet we did not know exactly how to go about creating it. We would meet many hurdles in crossing over to a new way of living. We had to toil through individual and collective obstacles, which required important changes in us.

I was confronted with regaining my health, writing this book and bridging the gap (more like a canyon) between old ways of thinking and those that would bring true success and happiness. Desirée and I both had to shift gears to realize our personal power and confidence. We needed to let go of our real estate plans (at least temporarily), move, change careers and start over. This was all part of our makeover, the stuff of the fourth dimension of wealth creation called clearing.

Vast changes may not be required of everyone who engages the clearing process, but usually some change is necessary to become unstuck and get on track with living your passion and Wealth Inside Out. Clearing brings about many benefits such as opening the gateway to fresh understanding and new ways of thinking. Most of us repeat over and over the same thought patterns based upon the beliefs we hold. This, in turn, drives our behavior and determines the results we get. Even a 5% change in our thoughts can make a huge difference.

Clearing also releases fear. It helps us identify hidden negative beliefs that hold us back and develop new empowering beliefs compatible with who we really are. We become more effective at engaging new skills to handle life's challenges. Clearing, in effect, gets us out of our own way and prepares us to fulfill our true wealth ambitions.

Many people try to avoid the clearing phase, saying it makes them uncomfortable and even more confused. But we can become so comfortable that it is difficult to contemplate change, even if the new direction we're after is better than what we may be holding onto. For example, have you ever ended a job or a relationship, or changed from a fixed way of thinking, and later looked back to wonder why you had held on? That is where we get the expression, "What was I thinking?"

Clearing often stirs us up. We may face our biggest fears and reevaluate closely held beliefs—our social and tribal programming. We may need to cultivate new skills or make changes in career, finances or where we live. We may also seek new friendships, spiritual direction and health regimes.

Clearing often leads to changes that stretch our comfort zone. Even reading about the topics of clearing and finding your purpose in life can rouse buried feelings and desires. However, to skip over this important dimension usually undermines our long-term success. A good way to think of clearing is as a personal and spiritual makeover. Even if we go through a period of discomfort, thereafter we strike a new course, one that we truly want.

My own period of discomfort got very real when I realized that the door to my purpose would not budge without exceeding my threshold of comfort. I needed a clearer path to the entryway, brighter lights in the corridor and softer music playing in the background. That is, it might mean a remake of my worldview and lifestyle, indeed even of my emotional wiring. But whatever it would take, I was ready to dig in. I had received such tantalizing encouragement from the Wizard (despite nonstop rebuttals from Sneaky Pete) that I had to press on.

Keep in mind that the process of clearing is what gives rise to new opportunities, especially those that lead you to Wealth Inside Out. Therefore, I have devoted the largest portion of the book to clearing. It is really a matter of one's priorities. Are you willing to risk change for a life of true wealth and happiness?

Recognizing Old Beliefs and Fears

Reexamine all that you have been told...
dismiss that which insults your soul.
—Walt Whitman, American poet (1819-1892)

A good place to begin clearing is by looking at the beliefs and fears that stop you from having what you want. Simply uncovering them is the first step. Often, the ones that hold you back most are not so easy to recognize because they are hidden in your subconscious.

For example, my old beliefs had made it difficult for me to be comfortable with the idea of guidance. When I looked at the origin of these beliefs, I was able to see what had stopped me from following my true wealth dreams. Then I could shift gears and see new possibilities.

Does this mean there is actually a physiological basis for our gut instincts?

Everyone comes from a particular brand of social molding, and my early childhood had left its stamp. I searched my roots to understand why I thought the way I did. Maybe this would help open the door to my purpose. In many ways, I had a great childhood, and in others, I was left with certain abrasions. Both conditions would impact my life and how I thought.

I'm a Southern boy. I was born in Sewanee, Tennessee and lived in Monroe, Georgia until age 6. Then my family moved to Alexandria, Virginia for three years before finally settling in Charlottesville, Virginia. My dad grew up in Georgia, and my mom, in Texas, so even my genetic encoding came mostly out of the South. A traditionalist frame of mind permeated the local people, and as I looked back I could see this influence from my family environment as well as from early teachers and mentors.

I felt a certain stability having our family intact, meaning that my parents stayed together. I grew up with two brothers and a sister; I was third in line. We went to good schools and were instilled with respectable values. We had fun times on family outings, vacations and visits with extended family.

This might appear to be the ideal American family, but an underlying tension at home affected my ability to be at ease. Like most people, I experienced certain events from my childhood as painful. With my parents juggling the responsibilities of work, marriage and parenting, we kids had too much unsupervised time and often looked for mischief. My older brother and I fought a lot, and he usually won. Many times I ended up the scapegoat, punished for what I had not done.

This kind of family quarrel might appear like ordinary sibling rivalry, but the disconnection it brought, as well as my parents not doing enough to stop it, affected my self-esteem for many years. I formed many erroneous beliefs about myself and about life, relationships, work and money. Beliefs like "I'm not good enough," "Something must be wrong with me" and "Relationships are unsafe" found their way into my subconscious. Some of these same dynamics later played out in a few of my relationships and with my career choices and the way I handled my finances.

What were the tensions in your family? What events may have seemed ordinary at the time but when you look back, are still painful? From childhood, we form beliefs about ourselves and about how life works. How many negative beliefs do you carry today that were birthed early in life?

Regardless of how happy you were while growing up, if you ever struggle with self-esteem, you can be sure that you formed erroneous beliefs about yourself at a young age. You may find yourself thinking things such as, "I'm not enough," or "I'm not valuable," or "What I have to say is not that important." Logically, you may know these statements are incorrect, but when you think about them, you feel awkward and know that the words ring true. The good news is that there is a powerful way to eliminate these debilitating beliefs. You will learn more about this as you continue reading.

On the fun side of childhood, my construction ability first began when I joined with other neighborhood kids to build forts with scrap materials "commandeered" from nearby building sites. Thirty feet up a tree, we would put up a fort and dig another down below that eight feet underground. Then we made one across a creek, accessible only by a hand-rigged drawbridge. One fort was fashioned from cinder blocks and cardboard, and another from wild bamboo. It was quite exciting, all these forts. We would camp out in them and hold secret meetings;

and when we got finished with one fort, we would start another. At night we often sneaked out to go "cool catting," our code word for knocking on doors and then running to hide while we watched who would answer. Every now and then we would get caught, but that did not deter us much.

In a way, I grew up with two families. I spent a lot of time up the street at my best friend's house. Bobby and I hung around like twin shadows for many years, and I was often included in his family outings. Bobby's dad was a key influence and role model, and he always went out of his way to include me. His dad liked to break the rules of the status quo and encourage us to think for ourselves, to each be his own person.

My dad was more reserved. Though they had different styles, both men embodied uncompromising integrity and valued family bonds. I'm proud to have grown up within this fundamental structure of loyalty, where I learned to face life's demands responsibly.

What role models did you most enjoy? Can you see a link between your early influences and the way you are today? Also look at your early interests and hobbies. What skills did you learn that may have shaped the choices you made later?

Charlottesville, a conservative college town located in Thomas Jefferson country, is a beautiful place. It is full of small town charm and surrounded by the rolling foothills of the Blue Ridge Mountains. It still has a revered connection to colonial times. There I learned to admire common sense and academic status, yet I was not very interested in traditional schoolwork so I often felt out of place. It is easy for anyone to feel this way in an environment where others are defining what is most important. In other words, if you are not on the same page with the rules of your environment, you may feel out of sync and even as if there is something wrong with you.

My autonomous nature against the backdrop of these childhood influences left me with the pull to venture beyond the bounds of Charlottesville. At 21, I moved to California, where I felt much better suited among those who welcomed new ideas. Even so, I often fought with myself while trying to break from the restrictive aspects of my upbringing. Some of my most limiting thoughts clearly reflected my responses to early influences and made it difficult to trust the new.

This was only clear to me much later when as a young adult I would visit Charlottesville. My interest in human potential and mind-body disciplines were somewhat frowned upon by the locals.

What was it like where you grew up? Did the societal mores of your locale fit with the way you truly thought and believed, or did you adapt to the status quo so you could fit in? Does the same mold still fit you today? What is something that you have always wanted yet feels out of reach because of the constraints you hold from your past? I am not saying that the values you grew up with are bad, only that they may not be truly yours. What would you need to do differently to step forward with greater confidence in a newly-inspired direction?

When I thought about my own resistance to change, it seemed related more to fear than anything else. After my first encounters with guidance, for example, I might have looked merely tentative. But really I was afraid to let myself go. What if I lost control over my life or was led toward something I didn't want? I was not so confident that the same organizing principle that had shown me the buffalo would continue leading me down the right path. Just when I had nearly lost my way, I learned more about why past imprints and programs need to be cleared before the new can fully develop.

Unlocking Your Neural Equipment

Brainwash yourself before somebody nasty beats you to it.
—Rob Brezsny, American writer

An important phase of clearing is to release what blocks us from being open to new ideas. Ordinary logic can make us believe we are seeing things clearly even when we are not. What goes on in our neural circuits during a logic-based process is entirely different than what takes place during the intuitive, subconscious process. Releasing blocks to success therefore requires a change in our neural architecture, which can happen by shifting patterned thought habits.

We tend to think we are the way we are and "that is just how life is." But how much of the way we are is a result of our unconscious neural imprinting? Repeated thoughts cause neurons in the brain to form patterns that further reinforce identical thoughts. Once formed, the neurons have an easier time repeating the same patterns than creating new ones. This means that you have to work harder (at first) to generate new thoughts than to keep rethinking existing ones.

The ways we are taught to think and believe thus become ingrained in our neural network even if we do not agree completely with what we were taught. So it may seem difficult to make the changes we know deep down would make our lives work better.

I was taught to be skeptical about the unexplainable aspects of life. Belief in things not yet "proven" was for the naive and the gullible. It was for all those "weak people who can't think for themselves," as I once blurted out. For a long time, I had bought into this kind of reasoning, but now I felt something new. I started to look at what science could not yet explain and at how many times authorities had been wrong. After all, everybody knows the earth used to be flat and the idea of going to the moon was ludicrous.

So, why does our culture often view the intuitive and spiritual nature of life with less importance than the thoughts generated by its logic? And how can we rely on science as an ultimate authority even though much remains unknown? It is a timeless misunderstanding that if today's science is unable to prove something, it must not be viable.

It is no secret that science is constantly upgrading information and making new discoveries. For example, it was reported by a university professor that just over a hundred years ago, in 1904, the following were U.S. facts: The average life expectancy was 47 years, 95% of all births took place at home, and only 6% of all Americans had graduated from high school. The average wage was 22 cents per hour. Marijuana, heroin and morphine were all available at corner drugstores and considered health enhancers. The population of Las Vegas was 30. No more than 8% of homes had a telephone. There were only 8,000 cars and 144 miles of paved roads. 90% of all U.S. physicians had no college education. Instead, they went to medical schools often condemned by the press and the government as "substandard" (this list attributed to Dr. Joseph Mercola).

In only 100 years, so much has changed, and changes are expected to continue at even faster rates. It is important to upgrade our internal software to keep current with what is actually true. Otherwise, we may make important decisions that are not up to date with present reality.

Even the term *software* did not exist a few decades ago. To recognize how we are affected by changing technology is the first step. For example, it has been only in the last few years that science has begun to understand how the brain functions in relation to emotions and how our actions respond to our beliefs. Not being able to apply this knowledge, however, will leave us at a disadvantage, thinking we are merely set with the lives we have. We can get stuck even when we know deep down we are capable of much more. Yet, learning how to reprogram our neural networks can change all of that.

The next step toward truth is clearing old programs to allow your intuitive nature to feed you accurate data. How many times have you gone against your gut instinct only to find out later that it was correct?

Research by the Institute of HeartMath in Boulder Creek, California uncovered three major neural networks in the body. Science has long been aware of the neural networks in the brain, which is the largest of the three, but there are two others. One is in the cardial sack, and another in the intestinal tract. Can we really be heartsick? And is there actually a physiological basis for our gut instincts? It would seem so.

For example, when Desirée and I put our apartments on the market, we got an offer, which we countered more than once. Each time that it came back from the prospective buyer, it was closer to the terms and price we wanted, but in my gut, I didn't have a good feeling about it. Logically, we became convinced that we had a good buyer who had all the necessary qualifications and so forth. The deal looked good on paper, so we eventually signed the contract. Three months later when they cancelled, I wasn't surprised. My gut instinct had fed me accurate data. Within days of this cancellation, we had a new contract from a different buyer, but for less money. Nonetheless, something felt very right about it. There was a sense of ease and a flow, so we moved forward with the deal.

I was talking on the phone with my mom one day, and she shared a story from when I was a baby. We were staying with relatives, and I was napping in another room with my siblings while my mom visited family. At one point, Mom had a strong instinct to check on us. "I immediately jumped up, saying that I needed to go check on the children," she recounted. Not expecting to find anything unusual, she came in the room to find me choking on a plastic ring that had pulled loose from a pacifier. "My instinct was different than my ordinary thought to check on the children," she explained. "But only in hindsight did I realize how intense it was."

So what does it cost us to be disconnected from our source of inner wisdom and intuitive clarity? What is the price we pay in terms of our health, natural expression, community and sense of connection to the greater whole? It seems we come into life already connected, but our environment deprograms it out of us. False programs installed during childhood can, in effect, cost us our very lives.

As I explored these ideas, I was slowly but surely (and naturally) beginning to clear old limitations. My focus began to shift from disbelief to curiosity about the idea of guidance and interior knowing. I wanted to know more about how our intuitive nature connects us with the greater whole. Really, how can we be separate from the source that causes life?

Even a scientific idea like the big bang theory of how the universe came into existence requires some organizing force to cause a precise environment for life to exist. Would anyone suggest that all the millions of relationships between time and space, and gravity, and temperature and chemical composition of air and water are a mere coincidence?

I began to reason that if all of these precise connections sustain our very survival, there must also be a purpose for each of us within this matrix of relationships. I began to see just how much my old thinking had held me back. I wanted to have a direct experience with *my* purpose. What unique contribution did I bring to the matrix?

Now take a look at the particular contributions you bring to life. What would bring true wealth and happiness to your daily experience and how would this help others?

Science without religion is lame, religion without science is blind.
— Albert Einstein, German-born physicist (1879-1955)

No one completely knows how the universe works. Sometimes we are happily surprised when science and wisdom traditions agree, but the knowledge of many things remains hidden from our logic and reasoning alone. There seems to be a higher order in the cosmos, and the progression of events often unfolds in ways we don't understand. But not being able to explain something through rational deductive reasoning does not mean it has no merit.

This idea can make us uncomfortable because we want to be certain. We want to know. We prefer placing definite parameters around reality because it makes us feel more secure, even when these boundaries may choke off other aspects of our being. We seek the illusion of being certain, yet how much certainty do we actually have?

Bridging the Gap
Overcoming Cognitive Dissonance

It ain't what you don't know that gets you into trouble.
It's what you know for sure that just ain't so.
—Mark Twain, American humorist (1835-1910)

The Wizard and the great organizing principle were showing me retreats and telling me to write books. Yet, from my old frame of reference these ideas seemed unlikely. Even while I was opening to new information and clearing away the old, I was buffeted by the effects of what psychologists call "cognitive dissonance."

An important aspect of clearing involves bridging the gap between our current beliefs and our new possibilities. When first receiving new information, our brain scans its memory database to find an existing frame of reference. If it finds none, one of three things will happen. I call these three things *balancing factors.*

One way to balance is to discount new information altogether; we say something like, "What a bunch of hooey." Another way is to reframe new information in terms we can understand, even if this reframing is incorrect. In other words, we filter incoming data through existing beliefs that may not be true factually. And the third way is to expand our understanding of how things work. This requires that we suspend existing beliefs for a period of time so we can look clearly at new possibilities. This does not mean that we should sacrifice our discernment when making important decisions; only that we will learn to look beyond our current circumstances to improve our lives when we are open to new ideas. Suddenly, fresh ways of viewing a situation come into focus.

> Rather than wondering if inner guidance is weird, focus on whether the guidance will take you where you want to go.

Which of the three do you tend to do? For example, how many times while reading this book have you felt the urge to discount or filter what you read?

The opportunity is always to expand, which takes place naturally when you learn to observe the process. In other words, start to notice what you do with new information or with ideas that may not fit within your ordinary viewpoint.

The greater the cognitive dissonance, the more uncomfortable we will become until one of the balancing factors kicks in, bridging the gap between what we *believe* is true and whatever may be challenging those beliefs. My journey became centered on exploring the edges of this discomfort as I moved nearer the dreams of my heart, allowing the process to propel me toward my true wealth purpose and Wealth Inside Out.

When there is a large degree of dissonance, our bodies produce neural chemicals that keep us from taking action. Not understanding this initially, I was unable to see that I was looking to my future from a context still based upon old ways of thinking. The vision I had about the retreat center was larger than what I would have ordinarily dreamed up. Writing books was also a major stretch. The dissonance between my old reality and the emerging one is what made me feel confused and kept me from taking action.

To reconcile the dissonance, Sneaky Pete would make discouraging comments like, "What kind of crazy idea is that?" At the same time, the Wizard showed me more possibilities. I seemed to fall somewhere in the middle, trying to reframe my experience in terms I could understand. You can see how I bounced between the excitement of the new and my fear about how it would all work out.

As I asked for inner guidance and clarity, I noticed another kind of dissonance. I felt a growing sense of obligation to follow the detailed answers I had asked for and received. I felt it was my duty to make "perfect" decisions.

I was afraid I would step into a mission beyond my capabilities or disappoint the Wizard, not to mention look irresponsible if things didn't work out according to guidance. I wondered whether the retreat center was to become a physical reality or might it be a metaphor for the direction my life needed to go.

Everything about our lives was changing, and we were clearing on so many levels that I had difficulty keeping up at times. I was overwhelmed. One day Desirée joked, "Certainly guidance must come with some sort of cosmic insurance," her way of saying to have faith in our intuitive wisdom. But with our whole life in upheaval, it felt more like cosmic shock therapy.

As I became aware of the dissonance, however, my questions shifted from wondering if this was weird to whether guidance would take me where I wanted to go. And my quest seemed to be leading toward the sense of purpose and wealth creation I was seeking. I only needed to find comfort with what was inevitably happening anyway.

The Power of Intention

Many outcomes happen by the conscious intentions we set. After the buffalo experience, I began to ponder more fully the organizing principles of life. I wanted to know how we come to live in harmony with these principles. How could I be in sync with the fundamental laws of life and my conscious intentions? I had said show me buffalo, and buffalo appeared. So it seems that this organizing principle responds to our internal intentions.

Intention is often considered a focus for *driving* ourselves to act or a rigid commitment of will. For me, however, intention was something inside that *wanted* to come forth. But it is not possible to do this when one is busy trying to *make* everything happen. This leaves no room to interact with a more fundamental reality—allowing one's natural expression to find its way. I was finally beginning to follow the Wizard's advice and let go.

> If indeed we have an inherent blueprint that seeks expression, it would certainly begin to surface from within.

As my intentions shifted from money concerns to a greater desire, I wanted most to know and experience life's essential unity. How did I fit into the bigger picture of humanity? Rather than continue my search only through logic and planning, I set an intention to allow my true wealth purpose to emerge on its own. If indeed we have an inherent blueprint that seeks expression, it would certainly begin to surface from within. By getting clear on my purpose, I knew I would create all the wealth I wanted financially, interpersonally, physically and spiritually.

I wondered if the organizing principle that responds to intentions might respond also to other motives I was not aware of. What hidden intentions might I have that were affecting my outcomes? It seemed the best way to know was to look at the results in my life. This would be the reality check of how I was thinking.

To create the kind of wealth and happiness you are seeking, your intentions must be clear. Otherwise you may find yourself feeling lost and unsure. For example, with clearer intentions, Desirée and I would never have been interested in many of the businesses we had explored. We were looking only at the financial aspects of our dreams without regard to what would feed our hearts and spirits. This same dynamic occurs with those who stay in a toxic relationship. The relationship may meet certain needs, but if it does not nourish the spirit, it becomes a drain. It is important to spend time doing what you most enjoy—emotionally, psychologically and spiritually. If you find yourself not liking something about your life, maybe it's time to take a deeper look. What is it that you want most of all?

To gain greater clarity, you can set an intention to receive clear understanding about your direction. What if you followed your inner whispers without being so concerned about what actually happened? Might you discover something new? Next, I'll share some of the ways I learned to do this via trial and error and more of my conversations with the Wizard.

Making Way for Letting Go

I began talking at length with the Wizard, telling him that in spite of everything, I was still afraid about selling the apartments. Desirée and I had financial goals based on real estate; why were we being led away from this?

> You must set your intention on letting go. Continue deciding to let go. Expect to let go. Commit to letting go.

The Wizard engaged me mightily on this one issue:

Yes Mark, you would do very well in real estate in Oklahoma City, but this will not fulfill your purpose or bring you the kind of wealth and happiness you desire.

"Well," I countered, "I'm not seeing a tangible opportunity in the new direction. Can't we keep our apartments while we pursue other dreams?"

There is ample opportunity for you, but you must first let go of what you have. From there everything will open.

"That seems difficult," I persisted, "because selling our apartments at this time goes against everything we've been taught about creating wealth and financial security."

You will have both financial security and the work you love. But for now, you will need all of your attention on the opportunity awaiting you.

"I need to see something concrete," I demanded, "or another sign that removes all of my doubt."

Yes, I will work something out for you.

The next night I had another prophetic dream about discarding outgrown attitudes and beliefs and opening to a higher understanding. I was in touch with my real potential and could sense a destiny to fulfill.

"Wizard," I said, ready to listen, "please communicate with me today. I got your message from the dream, but I'm still confused. My life seems kind of surreal, as if I'm lost in some faraway place in a distorted dreamland. Please talk to me again."

You need to let me communicate more freely and easily. Stop trying to control guidance and when I talk with you.

"I stop it only because I get overwhelmed." I responded, "You keep telling me to let go and to build a retreat center in Hawaii, sell our apartments and write books, yet how do you expect me to do all of these things? And besides, I want to have some say in all of this. I'm not seeing the way to replace our income. I want to trust this process of following guidance, but it's not like we have a long track record for me to go on."

It is difficult for most people at first, following guidance. In the beginning, it requires a bit of blind faith and trust. As things begin to work out, you'll build a history of experiences that give you increasing confidence. Right now, simply let go and trust. Once you let go of your apartments and stop fretting about it, you'll free up tremendous energy. Get what help you need to let go.

"How do I let go?"

You must set your intention on letting go. Continue deciding to let go. Expect to let go. Commit to letting go. Much of what you need to know about your direction, you are unable to see from where you are right now. As you let go, more and more clarity will come.

"Sometimes I feel like I'm going crazy having this kind of conversation," I said. "Do you really exist, or is this just me talking to me?"

What most people fail to understand is that your higher self and the voice of guidance are one and the same. When you talk to the infinite, you are actually talking with the part of you that knows. This conversation connects you with universal mind, which interacts with everyone and all of creation.

"So exactly what do I do next?" I said, having no comeback to that.

Sell your apartments and move to Hawaii.

"So are we done here in Carmel?"

Yes, you are done. You need only to wrap up any unfinished business and prepare for moving. Just keep letting go. You already know what you need to do.

The next day, Desirée and I talked about the timing of selling the apartments, thinking that maybe we should delay another couple of months to push the sale into the next tax year. That night I dreamed about a house that collapsed as it was blown over by the wind. *Wind* is about change, and *collapse* is about undermining of the self. "Pay attention to what is called for," was my message. Then in the early morning hours the Wizard spoke.

Don't wait to sell your apartments. Get things moving. Don't worry about the taxes.

When I woke up, Desirée's first words were, "Mark, we can't wait any longer to sell the apartments." Soon after, we called our broker to go ahead and list the units.

Later that day, Desirée was flipping through an album of the buffalo I had photographed during our trip to Oklahoma City. There was a picture I had taken of our apartment buildings from the freeway. I had exited immediately upon taking the snapshot and was not sure it would even turn out. As Desirée now looked at the photograph, she discovered a shiny golden buffalo statue on the parcel adjacent to our apartment buildings. Neither of us had seen this until that moment nearly three weeks later.

> You can use the following phrases to ask for inner and outer help: "Please help me open to my highest calling. Help me release the blocks, fears and beliefs that are in my way."

So there I had a confirming dream, an instruction from the Wizard, corroboration from Desirée and now another buffalo—all validation that I was on the right track.

You can see how the guidance we seek is all around. When you ask for help from the infinite, answers may come in many forms.

You can ask for a sign whenever you want confirmation. Something like "Infinite creation, please give me a sign that I will recognize as meaningful to confirm that I am on the right track," will work just fine. You don't need to ask for a specific sign. Then notice what happens around you during your normal activities, in your dreams and in symbols of the day. Pay attention to the people you meet and the things they say.

I continued asking the Wizard about my next steps. "I am not feeling connected with the retreat center nor am I sure how to begin writing. Again, I need to understand how I will make money to pay my bills...."

You need to surrender. To be fully integrated, you need to quit thinking so much. There is a place for you. Stop wasting energy on the thoughts and feelings as if you are missing out on opportunity. Hold onto the knowing that there is a place for you.

"Well," I said, "I need clarity about my purpose in life. Exactly what is my purpose?"

Your purpose is to help other people know their purpose. This will happen through your books and retreat programs.

Finally something clicked, and the idea of surrender actually registered. In an effort to let go and strip away my limitations, I looked in the mirror and said, "Mark, what if what you think you know is not the way things actually work? What if you don't know anything? What if you really did let go?"

This was my way of surrendering as I began reevaluating every assumption I ever had. That night I could feel my body unwinding during my sleep.

"Okay, Wizard, I surrender. I relinquish my ego, my knowledge and my arrogance to an ever greater knowledge. Please help me open to my highest calling. Help me release the blocks, fears and beliefs that are in my way. Help me understand how to create wealth from the inside out."

You are here to create retreat programs for helping others find true success and happiness. Don't let anyone tell you that you can't do this. The ball is in your court.

Following Guidance With Faith and Trust

You've got to go out on a limb sometimes
because that's where the fruit is.
—Will Rogers, American humorist (1879-1935)

My tug of war with new ideas offered by the Wizard went on for several months before a new direction took hold. Meanwhile, I was assisted in my makeover by some spirited friends who gave of themselves as I continued my journey. Everything conspired to open the way for our eventual move to Hawaii and the realization of dreams Desirée and I held dear.

▶ Don't Plan, Just Explore

Since the ball was now in my court, certainly we would need a good business plan. Through a mutual friend, we were introduced to Lori Wood, a Wharton MBA who consults with companies on strategy and planning. We invited her to lunch and shared our vision of the retreat center and experiences with guidance and the buffalo. I thought she would confirm that we had lost our marbles. But something else happened. As I was telling her the story of the buffalo totem, I noticed tears rolling down her cheeks. I asked, "Why are you crying?"

"I'm so moved because your story put me in touch with my own dream of running a residency retreat program for artists," she said. Our conversation has made me realize that I too can ask for guidance, that I have cut myself off from this resource and now I feel like I have it back. Thank you for sharing your story."

That's interesting, I thought. Here I am talking with an MBA about guidance and buffalo totems and she actually gets it.

Ready to move on with business and follow a commonsense approach, I expected Lori would advise us to begin planning and raising seed capital for the venture. What she said instead took me by surprise. "Don't put together a plan yet. Begin by talking with people about your vision and let some excitement build around the idea."

Lori told me later that in all her years of consulting, she had never advised anyone not to do a business plan. Without a plan, I wasn't sure what to do, so I asked the Wizard, "What's next?"

You will be a destination retreat center. Don't worry about the money. All that you need will be provided. Keep focused on your dream. This is your soul's purpose. Keep reaching out. Your pre-embedded clarity and confidence are unshakable. Practice meditation everyday. Stay away from people who drain you. Hawaii is your place. Many people will come. Keep trusting. Keep clearing. Keep going.

"How in the heck is this going to happen? And how do I deal with my paralyzing fear?" I felt panic rising again.

Just keep following synchronicity and energy. To release your fear, breathe in and on the exhale, let your fear unleash from your body. Then shift your focus. Remember your unshakable confidence. You'll be near Parker Ranch [a large cattle ranch on the Big Island]. *Go to Hawaii and explore.*

A few weeks later, Desirée and I made a two-week visit to Hawaii. Both of us were drawn to the hills above the town of Waimea and to the North Kohala coast, where I had never been before. After visiting there, we each felt a connection to the area. The landscape and views matched the visions I had been having. We loved the stillness, and the surroundings there made an impression.

We came upon Lapakahi State Historical Park, where we spent several hours talking with one of the guides. At one time, we were told, it had been a thriving village of fishermen and Hawaiian healers. We connected with the healing energy and wanted to embody this kind of feeling in our retreats.

A few days later, we toured the well-known Parker Ranch, once the largest private ranch under single ownership in the United States. Its history began in 1809 when a 19-year-old sailor named John Parker jumped ship and hid until his vessel left the island. He ended up with land through a connection with the great King Kamehameha I, who had fought to unite the islands into a single kingdom. The last heir to Parker Ranch was Richard Smart, who died in 1992. He set up a trust to provide continuous support to its four beneficiaries: two local schools, a community hospital, and a foundation trust.

Through our education at Parker Ranch, Desirée and I also learned about the meaning of *Kamuela*, the inspiration for our new business name, Kamuela Holistic Resort. We learned the Postmaster General had named the Waimea post office after the popular Colonel Sam Parker, one of the early heirs of Parker Ranch. *Kamuela* is the Hawaiian name for Samuel, which means "God listens."

There I was pondering the idea of guidance and wondering if life does indeed respond to our internal intentions. To find that we had coincidentally called our retreat center a name meaning "God listens" was truly remarkable.

While still on the island, I wrote the following "Divine Spirit" prayer, which I said each day to foster new levels of clarity.

Divine Spirit,
Bless me with your presence.
Show me what I am here to do.
Give me the wisdom to know
and the courage to follow inner guidance.
Fill me with your energy
and the vitality to fulfill my purpose in life.
Protect me from harm along the way.
Eliminate every thought in me that
is in the way of true success and happiness.

Continue taking the next steps, and all that you need will be provided. This is your soul's purpose. Work with those who will support your vision. All that you need will be given. Keep letting go. Keep trusting.

"How will all of this happen?" I asked.

Hear the birds outside? How do they know how to chirp? How do they navigate thousands of miles in migration every year? This is the kind of intelligence that will create your retreat center. It just happens when you don't stand in the way. Only you are your biggest obstacle. You must get out of the way and shift into pure creative flow....

Sneaky Pete chimed in with his usual sarcasm, "Yeah right, Mark, just tell Ol' Wizard you need a few million dollars, and someone will surely write you a check. Then go down to the planning department and tell them God sent you."

I did my best to ignore these comments. The next day the Wizard offered more food for thought.

Today is for matters of the heart. When the heart is open, the mind is calm. Your retreats will be a place of peace where hearts open easily.

After our time in Hawaii, we headed back to the mainland as planned. We had loved being in the tropical weather and swimming in the clear blue ocean; we had felt at home there.

▶ Keep Listening for What Is Next

> *Somewhere out there is a unique place for you to help others—a unique life role for you to fill that only you can fill.*
> — Thomas Kinkade, American painter (1958-)

Back in Carmel, however, I temporarily lost my resolve to let go and trust. Every time I wrote down one of the Wizard's monologues, cognitive dissonance would happen yet again. It could take several days between messages for me to relax.

Although I had become comfortable with the process of journaling the Wizard's words, I wasn't always sure what to do with them. How could I be getting such instructions to do what seemed so far out of my reach? I did not get a clear picture of what to do next. I could just imagine going to investors and telling them that a Wizard had told me to build this place. I'd be the laughing stock of the decade.

Sneaky Pete of course concurred, but the Wizard did not exactly back off.

Stop thinking that your inner guidance is weird—and stop wondering if it is real. It is as real as you allow it to be. It is really quite natural to communicate with the higher self.

Your purpose is to give people a place of rest. They will come to learn their purpose and get in touch with their big dream.... Keep taking the next step.

Wealth creation seems difficult for most people because it's mainly about letting go. But there is no reason to be afraid. Wealth creation is a normal part of life once you understand how it is possible for anyone to achieve it. Just take one step at a time. Then you will know what to do next. Life gets easier that way. When you get confused, stop and reflect. Your answers will come.

The process of inner listening was telling me I needed to create a place of rest, and I had been doing this for myself for several months since my health ordeal. The upheaval had been a catalyst for the crucial changes I needed to make, and now I was excited about clearing. My energy level was better, but working at the computer still bothered me a lot.

Finally, I began writing as best I could. To circumvent the computer problem, I often wrote by hand and then read my words over the phone to a transcriber who would e-mail them back to me. Weaving in my personal story took some effort, but the words of the Wizard always flowed out with ease. Writing soon began to energize me. I was taking action and writing my book.

My days were filled with poignant moments from which I could gain clarity and inspiration. All I had to do was pay attention and a wealth of information was at hand. For example, Desirée and I visited my parents in Virginia over the Thanksgiving holiday. One evening I found myself captivated by a television segment on *60 Minutes*. It was about 12-year-old composer Jay Greenberg, who was studying at New York's renowned Juilliard School. He goes by the nickname Bluejay because, like the bird, he is small and makes a lot of racket. Greenberg can hear music playing in his head and is able to write it down to create an entire symphony. The experience, he said on the show, seems to come from his subconscious mind "at the speed of light," and what he hears is like the "smooth performance" of a finished work.

His parents said that Bluejay started drawing pictures of instruments at the age of 2. He actually drew a cello, asked for a cello and wrote the word *cello*. By age 3 he began to compose by turning pictures of cellos into notes on a scale. It was all he wanted to do.

It was very clear that this child prodigy had more than just talent. By the time he was 12, he had written five symphonies. Most talented composers write only five or six symphonies in a lifetime! How could this be?

Seeing this did two things for me. First, it confirmed how each one of us is an integral part of the greater whole of life, not separate from it. Some organizing principle beyond what we fully understand is at play. Second, it increased my curiosity about my own natural gifts that might be seeking expression. Again, what unique abilities did I bring to the greater whole? As you consider this question for yourself, what are the talents that come naturally to you? How can you begin living your passion right now?

When I woke up the next morning, the Wizard began talking.

Mark, you are like the young composer, only with your own set of unique gifts and talents. You are here to fulfill your purpose. The difference is that Bluejay knows his purpose, and you are unsure of yours. You are on the right track. Keep taking the next step, and everything will become clear.

Move beyond your ordinary logic. All of this will surely make sense later. Keep moving forward, and your world will open up in amazing ways. You can have anything you allow yourself to have.

Look back to twenty years ago. The things that you were doing then are only now becoming known to the masses. This will also occur with your new path. Whenever you feel afraid or unsure, just think of the Bluejay.

▶ Opening Further to Infinite Mind

Nothing happens to anybody which he is not by nature fitted to bear.
—Marcus Aurelius, Roman Emperor (121-180)

In the middle of my long discourses with the Wizard, I went to see Dr. Bill Little, a minister friend and scholar of spiritual traditions. He was also a physics professor at a renowned military school, so he had both scholastic and experiential knowledge with physics and metaphysics (beyond the physical).

I shared with Dr. Bill my experiences with guidance and my uncertainty. His perspective was that I had opened up a channel in my subconscious mind, which is where we gain access to information from the greater universal mind. We may be presented with an array of choices through the inner mind, but it is important also to allow our guidance to filter through our feeling and heart nature. This provides the clarity we need to make good choices using our conscious mind.

Said more simply, we get information from the infinite through the subconscious, use feeling and heart to crosscheck our information and then choose with our conscious mind.

Dr. Bill said that our purpose in life is often too big to fulfill by ourselves. We need the ongoing support of the energy that causes life and creation, which is the same energy that gives us guidance. Often, however, we tend to hang on to other agendas, trying to control every outcome. When we bump up against our human limitations, our efforts sometimes backfire, especially if we are holding negative thoughts and beliefs.

> End each request for help with a phrase that denotes a letting go.

We need to remember that in the divine mind, there are no limitations. There is no dis-ease, or lack. So we can ask for what we need through prayer and meditation, or by just asking for help from the infinite. Each time we turn everything over to the universe, we release the burden of having to figure it out.

Saying something such as "Please bring me the resources needed to fulfill my purpose" usually works. Even more specifically, we may say "Please bring me an editor for my book or an expert mentor who can help me build my business." Dr. Bill recommended I end each request with a phrase that denotes letting go, something along the lines of "Bring me this, or whatever in your wisdom is best."

I asked Dr. Bill about my role in the bigger vision. How was this to happen?

"Leadership," he replied. "The role of a leader is to hold the vision and delegate the specifics." He said to think of my leadership as a stewardship for higher purpose; it's like having a senior partner—one of infinite wisdom who is guiding you. He reiterated the importance of deferring to this source and not taking on a big vision alone.

Dr. Bill agreed that I should continue with my book, that it would be valuable to others. I left my meeting feeling encouraged and continued journaling the guidance.

The programs you and Desirée develop will benefit the lives of many. You will teach people how to become successful and how to achieve true wealth and happiness with greater ease and confidence. Some will discover who they are; others will find inner peace and happiness. Some will find rapid transition to be too challenging and will need to go more slowly. *Everybody will find his or her own pace.*

"Wizard," I said, "please help me find clarity regarding a large-scale retreat center versus developing our own programs."

Start with your own programs. This will give you the foundation needed for your next steps. You can keep it small if you wish, but the large-scale project will help more people. Keep your heart open, as Dr. Bill suggested. Your heart will guide you to where you need to land.

"What about my soul's purpose?" I asked. "Will a smaller-scale project fulfill that?"

All of this is one and the same—the books, programs and retreat center. Any and all of this will take you where you need to go.

Focus on living your passion and doing what you love, then delegate everything else. Remember, leaders hold the vision. Leaders delegate. Become a steward of the work, not a slave to it. You must choose a starting point. Only then can you begin to live your dream.

Creating New Beliefs

In any project the important factor is your belief.
Without belief there can be no successful outcome.
— William James, American psychologist (1842-1910)

As I have noted, one of the most crucial factors that determine outcomes in life is your beliefs. Finding your purpose in life and achieving Wealth Inside Out will bring all limiting beliefs to the surface for clearing. If you wish to do what you love and move in a new direction, your underlying assumptions must be congruent with the direction you want to go. Since most limiting beliefs are not in your conscious awareness, you must become resolute in clearing them. I've heard estimates that as little as 17% of the human brain is used at a conscious level. This means that the 83% of what you think, believe and do could be on autopilot.

Have you ever been driving and suddenly realized that several miles have passed without your recollection of where you have been?

During this period of no awareness, your subconscious took over while your conscious mind was busy with other thoughts. To have greater influence over patterned ways of operating, it is important to gain conscious access to your automatic drivers. One way is to ask yourself questions that interrupt habitual thought patterns. For example,

- What exactly are my underlying assumptions about life? Where did I get my beliefs about love and relationships, money, sex, religion, health, government and so on?

- Are my assumptions true, or did I adopt them from the way I was taught to believe?

- Do my current beliefs support the vision I have for my life?

There are other questions to consider as well. For instance,

- Do you believe that you are inherently good, or does a part of you have trouble accepting this as truth?

- Do you believe you will create the true wealth you most desire?

- In your heart of hearts, do you truly endorse the spiritual beliefs you were taught, or do you feel inauthentic with them?

- Do you believe in a greater organizing source, or do we as humans have ultimate control?

- And perhaps the most important question of all is, Are the beliefs you hold landing you where you most want to be in life?

Another way to gain access to the subconscious is through the simple practice of intentional focus. You can become aware of where your attention actually goes and, repeatedly, bring yourself back to the present moment. Such exercises may encompass a variety of techniques from sitting still, to breathing practices, to reciting a mantra (a repeated word or phrase), to mindful walking, for example.

There are many other techniques for clearing and tapping into your subconscious that are beyond the scope of this book. You will find more of them in the supplementary *Wealth Creation Workbook*, which you can find at our Website, and you will also learn more as you continue reading.

You might try any number of processes, from guided imagery, to affirmation, to deliberate shifting of your emotional state. The important factor is to become aware of unconscious patterns and replace them with conscious ones. If you are not sure what you need, simply ask for guidance and clarity about the best resource for your next level of growth. For instance, you may say, "Infinite intelligence, please show me what I need right now," and you will get an answer.

As I explored my questions about beliefs, the Wizard gave his perspective.

There is an ultimate necessity to align your personal will with divine will. This is how to find true success and happiness and get in the driver's seat with your life. The great news is that your Self wants only the best for you. It wants you to be free of self-imposed restraints based on limitations that were impressed upon you by others....

The brain is a powerful instrument and is easily programmed. Keep clearing old patterns around success, money and relationships, and you will think and behave in an entirely new way. You can now develop new beliefs and skill-sets for the wealth and happiness you really want. You can cultivate new friendships with people who support you and who you want to become. You can develop beliefs that fully sanction your authentic being.

Next, I wrote out two questions that would help me realize my purpose and achieve Wealth Inside Out. At first, I did not believe the answers I noted. But at least I was beginning to build beliefs that would help me succeed. The first question was this:

Regardless of my hidden beliefs, what is essentially true about who I am?

I came up with three answers:

1. It is reasonable to believe that I am inherently good.
2. It makes sense to me that my life matters.
3. I believe that I have an important message that will benefit others.

Stop now and review these questions with three answers that pertain to you. What do you know to be inherently true about yourself even though it may not *feel* true at first?

Our level of self-confidence is essentially what we believe deep down about whether we are good enough or how much our life matters. Those with low self-confidence tend to look at the future through a clouded lens. Those in touch with their inherent value, however, see life more clearly. I intended to continue fostering the latter.

Another trap where many people get stuck is in thinking that beliefs are facts. What is a belief? A belief is simply an idea, a conviction or principle. It is an assumption or distinction with which we base decisions and live our lives. Beliefs are really interpretations of what *we* see and hear.

The way we respond to our environment is largely a function of our beliefs. For example, if you believe "I can overcome any obstacle," a part of you will look for obstacles and challenges to overcome. This may show up in your life as always struggling, striving and overcoming. Everything may seem hard as you go about chasing all those obstacles to overcome.

On the other hand, if your belief is that "Opportunities come to me easily," or "Good things always happen to me," then your life will begin to reflect these beliefs.

Whatever behavior others may have displayed to you during childhood was about them and their own ability (or lack of) to handle their daily challenges. Perhaps they were dealing with a stressed-out boss, feeling overwhelmed, or had self-esteem difficulties or simply had not developed the skills necessary to respond well to children.

But the beliefs we form about ourselves are purely what *we* create. Incidents may have occurred where we made key decisions about ourselves or about life—based upon beliefs that were not true. Yet we have carried those decisions into adulthood.

Now, as adults, we get to begin again. We get to start over. *We* get to decide what we want to believe. For example, I choose to believe that our inherent value as humans is not negotiable. It is not up for debate. Our value is congenital and cannot be taken away. It is the starting place for where we belong in life.

The second question I asked was this:

What beliefs do I need for my book and our retreat programs to be a success?

Here, I came up with five answers:

1. What I have to say and teach has value to others.
2. I can find language to express my message in a way that reaches my audience.
3. The resources we need will come to us as we need them.
4. I will follow through with the projects.
5. Many people will purchase the book and attend our trainings.

Writing out my answers helped. The process gave me a kind of holding tank for the direction I was headed.

You can do these same exercises using questions that open up new possibilities for whatever direction you feel called to express. Take time right now to create some answers for your direction that will strengthen you. What do you need to believe about yourself and your direction so that you will be successful? Using questions similar to those I asked the Wizard, remember to keep seeking your own inner guidance and clarity as you move toward the dreams of your heart.

The next morning, I woke up with three more questions:

"What do I need to let go of today?"

"What else do I need to know during this time?"

"What is calling me today?"

The Wizard's repetition of the answers seemed necessary and reassuring. I had to trust that hearing the words over and over would reinforce my inner messages and help me drown out Sneaky Pete. I counted all the times the Wizard had told me to let go or surrender, and it was a huge number—over 100!

It is important to spend time clearing and letting go. When you do what you love, live your passion and fulfill the calling of your purpose, many wonderful things happen. First, you love waking up each day. You focus on what you get to do rather than what you have *to do. You feel alive, and life is fun. It does not mean that you won't encounter challenges, but there is an underlying ease.*

"Wizard," I said. "I feel strange writing these things about purpose; I don't have much experience with the subject. How do you expect me to be a teacher?"

Yes, Mark, this is how it works. Finding your purpose in life grows out of what you already know in your heart and soul. As you begin removing the blocks to being fully yourself, your interior knowing begins to find expression. You release the knowledge deep within your fundamental nature. Your mind shifts to new questions such as,

- *What is calling you?*
- *What is it that you know you have to do?*
- *What is it that you cannot "not" do?*
- *What simply must be expressed?*

This is how you find purpose. This is what you will teach others. Think about these questions and then feel *what* wants *to come forth from deep inside. Take off the brakes as you connect to the life you are here to live.*

Now you must choose. You can take the path of survival or the path of purpose and Wealth Inside Out. Let the walls come down from around you as you set aside your limitations, then see what opens.

I liked the idea of setting aside my limitations, and I was excited about moving toward my purpose. We also needed to focus on income; it appeared we still had some clearing to do around money.

A Matter of Money

Everything you value can be held within your purpose.
—Desirée Watson

Some people have difficulty with the topic of money, especially in the same conversation with the spiritual nature of life. Nonetheless, I began to see that the source that brings us guidance is the same source that leads us toward opportunities where we can make money. Remember that true wealth is about well-being. Wealth Inside Out includes every kind of wealth, financial, interpersonal, physical and spiritual wealth.

Many people are willing to do things for money that they do not love. What kind of wealth is that? Now I was looking for a way to follow my higher calling while getting paid for doing what I found joyful. I highly recommend you find a way to do the same.

All of us have a certain threshold or capacity for money based upon our beliefs. Whatever beliefs we hold about money will determine the amount of money flowing through our life.

Let's say, for example, that you are used to making $50,000 a year, which is your internal comfort threshold. Suddenly you begin making significantly less or more. Your comfort threshold will likely be triggered, causing you to feel uncomfortable. To reestablish comfort, you will almost automatically begin doing whatever brings your income back into balance with your threshold. If your income has dropped, you'll go make more. If your income increases, you may face new circumstances to cause such an increase to be temporary. Expanding your wealth creation abilities usually requires that you first expand your capacity, your internal comfort threshold for wealth creation. This requires clearing.

Begin by asking whether you know someone who makes less money than you and someone who makes more money than you while doing the same kind of job. In every industry, you'll find people who struggle with money and people who make millions doing something very similar.

Where do you find yourself along this financial continuum, and are you doing what you love in order to create money? If you don't like your answers, you must do some more clearing. The money and your true success and happiness can flow only to the degree of your internal capacity for prosperity and doing what you love.

Desirée and I had hit our threshold several times. We'd get to the ceiling of our comfort and inevitably backslide as we returned to our comfort range. Eventually, we would change all that.

It is easer to expand your capacity for wealth creation when you are aligned with work you love. Starting any new venture usually takes time, energy and resources. Doing what you love—something that lifts you out of bed each day—helps you persevere when the going seems tough. Following your inner guidance never leads to ignoring the necessity of money, which some people worry about. Only your limiting beliefs do that. People get in more financial trouble by ignoring their intuitive clarity than by using it. It gets their lives on track.

Your innermost wisdom always takes into account the whole of your life, not merely one aspect. If money is genuinely important, you will find resources to help you manifest this. You will get the message for things such as "Read that book about money," or "Take this class on investing," or "Call John Smith about a new business opportunity."

Listening to your heart does not mean you should disregard money. Everyone must deal with money—or the lack of it. Either way, your focus is still directed to money. Surely you must learn how to fund your dreams.

Money is a powerful resource and helps you maneuver through life. When you learn to create wealth from the inside out, your energy shifts and what you value most comes into focus. Be willing to do whatever clearing you need around money. Get the expert help you need to move forward.

Desirée and I could only begin helping others in this way once we let go of our grand plans. Only then did the true wealth opportunities we were seeking begin to open. Our financial desires didn't change, only the means by which we thought they were to come about. First, we needed to move into our ideal wealth creation niche, a focus that would feed us spiritually *and* financially.

Pursuing your dreams most often requires that you obtain specialized knowledge and training to be successful financially. If you are entrepreneurial by nature, your knowledge (and thus guidance) may be different than for those who prefer to serve within a corporate or organizational structure.

Desirée and I had to first let go of our focus on money to get in touch with purpose and how to be happy. Later, however, we were led to powerful mentors and teachers who would show us how to handle the business and financial side of our work. As our financial comfort threshold expanded, money flowed more easily and Desirée and I moved closer to our Wealth Inside Out destiny. Our beliefs about money had shifted.

The Wizard chimed in with his words of encouragement.

There is enormous social stigma around the subject of money, which is directly linked to the flow of life itself. Money is the blood supply of material life. Sure you can get by with only a little, but why not tap into this vast resource simply by clearing your unwanted beliefs about money.

Most people don't understand money and how it actually works in the real world. They sell only their time for money, which distorts their outlook on money by the boundaries of time. Selling time for money, without also setting up a way to leverage your efforts, constricts your view of what is possible.

Flow and abundance are completely unlimited resources. When you become aligned with this flow, your access to money also expands. Transform your underlying beliefs about money; otherwise, they will keep you stuck. There is plenty of money to support any vision or dream you may have.

Keep clearing your mind, Mark. It is safe to receive money. Remember the buffalo. You told the universe to show you buffalo. Now tell it to show you money.

Higher Self Rules

Keep away from people who try to belittle your ambitions. Small people always do that. The really great make you feel that you can become great.
—Mark Twain, American humorist (1835-1910)

By now, the Wizard and I had talked about money, limiting beliefs, fear, inner guidance, programming, cognitive dissonance, power, letting go, higher purpose and relationships. While clearing any issues I may have had around these topics, I began to experience many internal shifts. I opened to new ideas about how we can co-create with the natural laws of life, and I was doing what I loved by writing this book. Now, I wanted clear guidelines to distinguish between the voices of Sneaky Pete and the Wizard, as well as to identify my responses. Sometimes I couldn't quite tell who was talking.

Reading over my journal entries, I isolated the common characteristics of each inner voice. Sneaky Pete pressed me only to get by. The Wizard would talk about my purpose and how to live my passions and encourage me to go for it. Sneaky Pete's words made me feel discouraged, afraid and drained. When I listened to the Wizard, I felt energized and expansive. Sneaky Pete was judgmental and critical, while the Wizard was optimistic and supportive.

I assembled a chart [Table 1.] to reflect the fundamental characteristics of Sneaky Pete and the Wizard. Seeing their responses side by side, I could better see my choices. I could listen to Sneaky Pete, the critical, limited voice of my programming, or to the voice of the Wizard, my higher self and intuitive intelligence. I could contract or expand. Everyone has this same choice, regardless of what names they call their limiting fears and worries—or the dreams of their hearts.

Table 1

Who Will You Listen To?

Sneaky Pete The Voice of Limitation	Wizard The Voice of Possibility
...talks about competition and what you *have* to do to get by.	...talks about vision and your life's purpose.
...wants you to defer your joy and happiness.	...wants you to be happy right now.
...is scattered, makes you feel out of sync and boxed in.	...is consistent and becomes familiar.
...squashes your enthusiasm and drains you.	...leaves you feeling energized and expansive.
...uses fear to manipulate and makes you feel alone.	...is loving and makes you feel connected.
...is judgmental and critical.	...is optimistic and supportive.
...weakens you and your confidence.	...makes you feel empowered and gives assurance that you can do it.
...has an immature tone and is full of rationalizations.	...has a mature tone; is direct and to the point.
...tries to instill worry and fear.	...responds to prayer and requests for help.
...tries to make you feel bad about yourself.	...knows you are inherently good.
...makes you worry that you won't be able to make a living doing what you love.	...guides you toward getting money by doing what you love.
...sees you as uncertain and is full of "yes buts" and "what ifs."	...sees you as successful and encourages you to trust.
...says you don't have the right credentials or qualifications to begin your dream.	...encourages you to begin your dream now without knowing exactly how.
...says it's hard to imagine something this good could happen to you.	...says, "Why not you?" When you align yourself with purpose, doors open and miracles happen.

You can see from Table 1. that the higher self is plugged into the big picture, but not our negative thinking. Our connection with heart and spirit will lead toward our larger potential if we can only get out of the way.

The lower self at least presses us to handle our physical needs. But Sneaky Pete is stuck in thinking that's all there is. Instead, we want to move beyond mere survival into a life that feels *alive*. This becomes possible when our survival needs are aligned with our purpose. If we are not moving toward finding our purpose in life and living our passion, know that *we* are the ones blocking this.

Clearing allows us to move freely without the limitations of our past as we pass through a personal and spiritual makeover. Although we may bump up against our biggest obstacles, we must not make the mistake of allowing the very issues in our way to stop us from clearing them. My challenge was to get past thinking that I already knew the answers and then give myself permission to explore a new path.

Your inner guidance tells you where to focus at any particular time. Sometimes you are pointed toward a specific task or project and at other times, toward something as simple as taking a rest. You may need to deal with the unfinished business of your past or face your most prevalent fears. You may have a sudden urge to get in touch with a particular person, just to find that you unexpectedly run into her or him.

When you are open to your intuitive perception, you clear the way to your higher self and true wealth creation. New possibilities present themselves giving you new choices about how you live and finding true success and happiness.

Dottie's Story

Dottie came to me wanting to move forward on a business venture that involved a particular kind of consulting. She was making around $40,000 at a job she no longer wanted to do. Nearly all of her friends thought her consulting idea was ludicrous and that she could never do it. In fact, she later told me that I was the only one who told her that she could do it and that her idea would work.

After a few wealth mentoring sessions, I helped Dottie formulate a plan and clear the unwanted negative beliefs that had held her back. Three months later, she called me to say she had landed a $60,000 plus contract from her very first client for that particular program. Clearing her limiting beliefs allowed Dottie to begin living her dream.

Clearing

Points to Remember

- Clearing works like a personal and spiritual makeover. You may be uncomfortable at first, but stay with it as you set a new course for your life—one you truly want.

- Upgrade your internal software with programs that support where you most want to go in life. Are you open to the possibility that your life can work differently than you think?

- Remember cognitive dissonance and the three balancing factors. Before writing off a new idea that challenges your closely held beliefs, see if your current beliefs support what you truly want. Then you have choices.

- Become aware of your underlying assumptions about life, money and doing what you love. Are they accurate and do they support what you most want out of life?

- Pay attention to your conscious and unconscious intentions. Are they compatible with the kind of wealth you want to create?

- Consider what beliefs you need to hold for the life you most desire.

- Often the biggest part of clearing is simply letting go to trust the natural process of wealth creation. Try being present with your fear as you learn to let it go. Focus on how you can move toward your dreams?

- When you get scared, remember to breathe and ask for help.

- You don't have to do it all alone. Whenever you feel stuck, ask for inner guidance and clarity. Ask for what you need, then let go of your fixed agenda and how it will happen. Embrace life's natural organizing ability. Employ the guidance of expert mentors who will teach you how to become successful.

- Pay attention to your inner voices. Who is talking—your Sneaky Pete or your Wizard?

For more powerful exercises about clearing that will help you achieve wealth from the inside out, download your supplementary *Wealth Creation Workbook* at www.WealthCreationWorkbook.com.

The road to happiness lies in two simple principles:
find what it is that interests you and that you can do well, and
when you find it put your whole soul into it—every bit of energy and
ambition and natural ability you have.
—John D. Rockefeller, American industrialist and philanthropist (1839-1937)

Chapter Seven

CHOOSING

What Is Choosing You?

*Don't aim for success if you want it: just do
what you love and believe in and it will come naturally.*
— David Frost, English journalist (1939-)

When we choose a direction in life, we may think we are the only ones doing the choosing. And indeed, it is important that we make choices. However, sometimes we pursue directions that are not choosing us. If we just try enough or work harder, we can possibly force something to happen. This is one way to go about life, but the path of Wealth Inside Out is about getting in sync with our natural rhythm. Besides making an effort, we need to pay attention to how life is responding.

When stepping into your purpose in life, the efforts you make have a reciprocal quality. What you put out comes back to refuel your next efforts. As you move toward what is *calling* you, pay attention to what is *choosing* you.

On the flip side, you may not want the situations that choose you. To understand why, begin to examine your intentions and the internal forces that generate your outer experiences. You may be unconsciously choosing situations you do not want. With more awareness, you can do what clearing is needed to choose anew. Of course there are times one must persevere in the face of life's challenges. But the path of Wealth Inside Out is fueled by a fundamental clarity in direction, and you will be energized by your persistence. So it is important to pay attention to your energy and the way life is rewarding your efforts. Take a moment now to reflect upon your level of energy for what you are doing. Does your work fill you up or drain you? Do your relationships fill you or drain you? Does your life direction fill you up? Are you moving toward true success and happiness?

An Unsettling Dilemma

A bird does not sing because it has an answer.
It sings because it has a song.
— Chinese Proverb

As I was writing *Wealth Inside Out*, I was energized by my efforts to continue. The book was certainly choosing me. There was a reciprocal quality to it. Whenever I wrote, new thoughts emerged easily, and resources came together without difficulty. It was fun. However, when I began to weave my personal story into this section on choosing, I bumped into a rather unsettling dilemma. I hadn't yet chosen just what I was going to do next. Although I'd written down the Wizard's thoughts on the subject, my personal story was not yet resolved.

Obviously, I had chosen to write the book, but what about the retreat center? I had made strides toward this, but I was not particularly energized, and it was not yet clear whether a center would happen or not. You may recall from Chapter One that I began by writing this book out of sequence and contrary to the conventional and logical way. Without a conclusion to my story, I was now face-to-face with an incongruity. The sale of our apartments had not yet closed escrow, we had not moved to Hawaii, the book was not complete and we had not started our new wealth creation programs. How could I possibly write about choosing when I was still waiting for all these events to take place?

Talk about confusion! I was befuddled and unable to write for several days. Then I had another tête-à-tête with the greater powers that be, only this time I was slamming my pillow at the foot of my bed. During this ostensible act of irreverence, I released my pent-up frustration by demanding clarity. I wanted to move forward without feeling so hampered. As I explored further the idea of what was choosing me, I began to get clear.

Rethinking Commitment

The moment one definitely commits oneself, then providence moves too.
A whole stream of events issues from the decision, raising in one's favor
all manner of unforeseen incidents, meetings and material assistance,
which no man could have dreamt would have come his way.
— Johann Wolfgang von Goethe, German poet (1739-1832)

Desirée and I posted this quote by Goethe on our vision board, a large space we used for collages of whatever we dreamed about doing or having. Periodically, we change it, depending upon our focus. During our Wealth Inside Out transition, the board included pictures of Hawaii, a beautiful home, retreat centers and people, along with little quips and quotes we liked.

Most people think of commitment as *working hard.* If the desired result is not coming quickly enough, work harder. However, waiting until we know what to do next is sometimes the best way of expressing our commitment.

The Wizard had his own say on the matter.

It is important for you to pay attention here, Mark. Remember, true commitment is more about an integral state of being than a process of doing. You were raised with a strong work ethic; now it is time to develop your "being ethic." It is from here that you will have the most influence and you will ultimately be the most productive. Do not get caught up in excessive doing. Whatever work is needed will come to you as you simply focus on your objectives. From there, you will know when to take action and when to back off.

My energy began to shift, and I sensed a slow momentum moving me in a new direction. The impulse had its own power. It was as though life itself was choosing for me; my job was simply not to stop it. Instead of iron will, my new commitment was more about surrendering to what life already had in store. This kind of commitment felt good.

What kinds of commitments may be causing you to overwork? What are you looking to join together? Do you know when to take action and when to back off? In what ways are you waiting to move forward? Are you willing to take some steps forward now?

As a trial run to experience this new way of being, I decided to follow one of the Wizard's instructions. I wanted to see what would happen if I quit holding back.

Being With Fred

We are whole and complete. This is not a goal
we are seeking to obtain. This is the starting point.
—Fred Jealous, Founder, Breakthrough men's community

When Desirée and I were at The Crossings retreat center near Austin, Texas I was guided to "write books, write books, write books." You'll recall that one of the ideas was to write about being with Fred, my long-time mentor and friend.

Some fifteen years earlier, I had attended a program for men, developed by Fred Jealous. Fred envisioned men being able to connect with each other outside of the socially-conditioned male role—acting tough, not showing emotion, keeping a cool distance and so on. That is, young boys who have not yet been conditioned this way will tend to carry on a more gentle connection in relationships with other boys. Fred's work is about making room for the authentic expression we naturally have as men.

I spent a lot of hours with Fred in private consultation as I worked through some of the negative influence that Sneaky Pete then had on me. I had trained with other kinds of mentors, but never anyone like Fred. I believe the introductory quote exemplifies the way Fred thinks. He has an extraordinary way of hearing people. He embodies a distinctive presence, and he made a connection with me—a real connection. This wasn't just because I was paying him. He went the extra mile.

For several months now, I had pondered the Wizard's idea of a book called *Being With Fred*, but I was focused on writing *Wealth Inside Out*. Then what came was to ask people in Fred's larger community circle to contribute. Even this seemed like too much, but that gentle voice of the Wizard kept nudging me on.

One day shortly before Thanksgiving, I took off the brakes and called Fred's wife, Ann, to see about setting up a surprise event. Several hundred men had gone through Fred's programs. A sister program had been attended by many women. We got the word out through a series of mailers, asking people to contribute a few words or photographs that highlighted their individual experience of being with Fred.

People showed up in droves. Suddenly, I had a team helping with all the various aspects—communications, compiling book entries, finances and coordinating a surprise gala. Together we created a book of sentiments and then celebrated with Fred on Valentine's Day.

Fred was beside himself. Ann had told him that they were going out with his immediate family for a Valentine's dinner. Upon entering the room of 115 people, he stood for about two minutes not quite able to grasp how this surprise had come together. The room was beautifully embellished with flowers and other decorations. We were all standing in a big circle under a banner that said "Everybody Needs a Fred." His silence finally broke as the band began to play and people came up to share their gratitude.

That night during my sleep, I felt my body unwinding from the excitement and the satisfaction of being complete with the project. I also noticed an unusual letting go; a kind of discomfort was peeling off of me. Something about stepping into leadership with the project triggered a release of what had previously held me back. It was as if I was shedding old feelings of shame and embarrassment about simply being myself, yet there was a wonderful emergent quality to this experience.

I awoke the next morning in a state of remarkable calm. Suddenly, after eight months of fear and confusion, I felt confident and clear. I was compelled to take some action toward our retreat center vision. We set up our business structure in Hawaii and began developing our logo and corporate identity. I still wasn't sure exactly where my efforts would lead, but I was moving forward.

Look now in your own life. Is there a special goal or project that you've been waiting to begin? What do you think you life would be like if you stopped holding back and took action? How would it feel to achieve your goal?

What Flows Naturally

There are three rules for running a business;
fortunately, we don't know any of them.
—A. E. Hotchner, American author, *Shameless Exploitation:*
In Pursuit of the Common Good (1920-)

This is one of my favorite quotes because it captures the way situations often work in real life. Sometimes you can make all the "right" plans and follow the "right" rules and still not land where you want to land. Life seems to have a way of its own

> Remember, that your purpose in life is not about making up a purpose. It is about identifying the inherent gifts inside of you that are seeking expression.

with no guarantees of being logical or practical. Following the path of intuitive clarity will not necessarily lead you in a straight line, but if you can tune into what is actually flowing and move with that, it will lead where you need to go.

A. E. Hotchner is a business partner with Paul Newman for the Newman's Own food line. They followed an unconventional path to success, often going against the "best" advice. They never had a well-mapped plan, which they discuss in their book, *Shameless Exploitation: In Pursuit of the Common Good* (2003). This recounts their unlikely success story of building the Newman's Own company and giving away the proceeds (over $150 million) to charities. In addition, they set up a group of camps for children with terminal illnesses, again breaking all the rules. They relied heavily on their gut instincts and kept taking action in the face of overwhelming odds. It's an inspiring story.

Suddenly my rumblings for teaching came rushing forth with renewed vigor. I became less concerned about what form the retreat center might take and began delivering speeches in my mind about finding your purpose in life and true wealth creation. I had to begin conveying my message about true success and happiness and creating Wealth Inside Out.

By now, our apartments were in escrow, we had a flight booked to Hawaii, the Being With Fred project was complete and I was nearly finished writing this book. Desirée and I were choosing these things, and they were choosing us.

I was ready to be immersed in my new field of personal development in whatever capacity flowed naturally. I began helping others learn the skills of true wealth creation and how to become successful and how to realize their dreams. The Wizard kept me on track, helping me to understand my choices and encouraging me further.

Momentum From Your True Wealth Purpose

There is a time to let things happen and a time to make things happen.
—Hugh Prather, American author (1938-)

Yes, Mark, finding your purpose in life and true wealth creation are good directions for your first book, which will draw many people to you. There is indeed great power in finding your purpose and how you choose to create wealth. Knowing your purpose in life will focus you like nothing else. Your purpose is important because it affects everything in life for your entire life. It affects your happiness, the quality of relationships, the way you spend time and the situations in which you get involved. Without clarity, your energy goes here and there randomly. When you know your purpose in life, you know where you are headed.

As I took this in from the Wizard, I recalled an analogy I once heard about the difference between a light bulb and a laser beam. The light from a 200-watt light bulb is diffused over an entire room. The same 200 watts reconfigured into a laser can cut through a piece of two-inch thick steel. In the same way, clear focus cuts through your distractions. All your problems may not disappear, but they become less taxing.

Some people may say, "Well, I like what I'm doing for the most part, and I am focused in my life." Having a have focus does not mean you are aligned with true success and happiness. Again, are you living your passion for life? Does what you are doing fill you up or drain you? If you love what you are doing, and it is giving you energy, most likely you are aligned with a sense of purpose. You just may never have defined it in those terms.

Let's simplify the idea of purpose:

- Purpose is anything you love doing that gives you energy.

- Purpose is an inner knowing that you are here for a reason, and you become involved in activities that fulfill this reason.

- Purpose is the big dream inside of you, the one you've always longed for.

- Purpose is about helping other people in some way, either directly or indirectly, through your actions.

- Purpose feels good even in the face of adversity.

- Purpose provides clarity, focus and meaning in your life.

You could use these same descriptions for wealth:

- Wealth is anything you love doing that gives you energy.

- Wealth is an inner knowing that you are here for a reason, and you become involved in activities that fulfill this reason.

- Wealth is the big dream inside of you, the one you've always longed for.

- Wealth is about helping other people in some way, either directly or indirectly, through your actions.

- Wealth feels good even in the face of adversity.

- Wealth provides you with the resources you need to carry out your dreams.

You may ask, "Okay, if I have a purpose in life, how do I know what it is? How do I get myself aligned with it?"

You begin by setting an intention to become aware of your purpose and whether you are following it. This is often preceded by a realization that the life you've been living is no longer working. Are you headed where you want to go, or do you feel out of sync? If you feel like you are not aligned with your purpose, you probably aren't.

Ask yourself these questions:

- Do I like waking up in the morning to meet the day ahead?

- Do I feel full and alive and happy most of the time?

- Do I feel as if I have a choice about my life direction?

If you answered "no" to any of these, you are likely misaligned with your purpose. Well, you are not alone. But there is a way out. You don't have to live a life predestined to feeling stuck. You have choices.

What if true success and happiness are not as random as many people think? What if an intentional purpose exists for every living creature? Even if this idea cannot be proven, wouldn't it be fun to live each day with a sense of purpose, knowing how you fit into the greater matrix of life?

This is what happens when you do what you love and discover your purpose in life. But getting in sync with your direction is not usually done alone. There is help all around. You can become aware of the vast and unified field where all of creation begins. The infinite source is much bigger and more powerful than anyone can imagine. Many people have difficulty acknowledging the limitless resource underlying the universe, but if it did not exist, neither would we. The same power created the sun and the sky, the beautiful mountains and us as human beings. But even if you do not believe in this source per se, for the sake of living a more fulfilling life, why not find a way to expand your connection to life and the natural process of wealth creation and creating your dreams?

Now, simply ask for help from this great intelligence. Call it what you like: universe, flow of life, praying to God or whatever. Again, find the language that works for you.

Here is an exercise that opens up the receiver channels through which your purpose is revealed.

- Sit quietly for a few minutes with your eyes closed. Focus on your breathing. As you inhale, think of the unlimited life of the universe filling you up. As you exhale, allow your mind to empty.

- Now bring your attention to the source of all creation and say these words:

> I surrender my life to fulfill creation's intention for me.
> I ask for help from the universe to reveal my purpose.
> Please help me know my purpose in life.

- If nothing comes right away, continue asking every day, What's my purpose? What's my purpose? What's my purpose?

Remember, that your purpose in life is not about making up a purpose. It is about identifying the inherent gifts inside of you that are seeking expression. The clarity in your own system will reveal your purpose to you once you truly want to know it.

Using your free will, you can choose to synchronize yourself with the intention of life's will. This leads you to your special reason for being born. Choosing, therefore, is not based upon random wishes but upon a deep-rooted calling to express your true wealth potential. This occurs naturally when you remain connected with the deepest desires of your heart and soul.

Many people go through life doing only what they *have* to do or what they *feel* like doing. But the greatest vitality comes when your focus goes out in a way that comes back to you, giving you even more energy.

Shortly after writing these thoughts, the following messages came through from the Wizard. They encouraged me in the new directions I was going:

Mark, you can begin teaching this now. Remember your purpose is about helping others find their purpose and create wealth from the inside out. You will now manifest your dreams based on the intentions you have set. Continue asking for what you need, and it will happen. Keep working from the inside out as you focus on your vision and goals.

Decoding the Guidance

*Sometimes on the way to a dream,
you get lost and find a better one.*
— Robin Rawlings, American artist

Some inner messages are literal, and others are symbolic. At first, I made a lot of effort stewing over which was which, yet trying to figure it out only wore me down. I had to learn how to trust that clarity would come with time. For example, I had the unexplainable urge to build a retreat center, but all I knew for sure was that my direction would somehow involve retreats and trainings.

Inner guidance may not always lead where you think you are going. What matters is that you follow what calls to you. You will naturally learn how to decode your essential inner messages along the way, a process that is unique to each individual. Begin by allowing your intuitive perceptions to lead *toward* what is seeking expression. You may get a simple message, such as to call a friend or to help someone cross the street; or perhaps something outrageous may come up, such as to build a bridge across the Atlantic Ocean. And by merely moving toward these messages, opportunities will open—some that you may not even see coming.

Often we get stuck because we insist on knowing outcomes before we take action. So we wait, failing to go toward our true wealth dreams. But how could we possibly expect to know outcomes that are put in order by the more powerful organizing principles of life?

It is more useful to begin perceiving your internal blueprint for success by allowing this to find its natural expression. When you act upon your intuitive whispers, rumblings or inner guidance, you will be led naturally toward wealth from the inside out.

I'm not saying that you shouldn't make plans and goals, only that you need to unleash your natural passions and let them express. Plans and goals work best in the support of a clear passionate direction and what you most enjoy. Choosing is about moving toward your purpose without knowing (at first) exactly how it is all going to work out.

For example, when I first perceived the retreat center idea and began stepping toward that vision, my enthusiasm for this book and for creating retreat programs emerged on their own. It seemed almost like a cosmic trick. I had so much fear about the retreat center that I hardly noticed that I was writing book. My ordinary logic might have prevented me from writing without first having full clarity and completing my transition to Wealth Inside Out. But this *was* my transition. Much of the book was emerging, blow by blow, without me getting in the way.

I still wasn't sure whether my messages about Kamuela Holistic Resort were literal or symbolic, but I began to relax about not knowing. While moving toward my intuitive whispers, new opportunities would begin taking form. Or alternately, I would become clear on the symbolic purpose of the messages. Either way, I was already being led to writing and helping others create wealth and find true happiness. These outcomes alone were sufficient. I was moving forward with my purpose in life. I was choosing, and my true wealth purpose had chosen me.

Take a look at your own life. What are the situations that keep choosing you and are these the ones you want? Are you ready to follow your dreams? Are you ready to create true wealth in at least one area of your life, financially, interpersonally, physically or spiritually? What is choosing you now?

Emerging From the Void

*Commitment is more about an integral
state of being than a process of doing.*
— Wizard

From my endings and awakenings of the last year until I approached this dimension of choosing, I was held within the vastness of the void. A journey through the void can sometimes try our faith. We get weary and ready to move on. But you'll recall the void has a timing of its own. The most freeing thought you can have is that the void won't last forever. You don't have to force your way out. It truly is a natural part of the greater reorganizing system.

During the recalibration process that prepares you to follow your dreams and the life you most desire, you let go of the way things were. Don't worry if you have not yet found your purpose. The intuitive whispers choosing you will reveal whatever obstacles are holding you back and give you the opportunity to choose anew. Trying to resist or avoid the process only slows you down. With sufficient faith and commitment, however, the dreams of your heart become more important than your fear.

As my confusion began to lift, I could see the light at the end of the tunnel. I was excited about my new direction. Upon arriving at the choosing stage, I was like a baby ready to be born. I was leaving the womb and entering the birth canal to meet my purpose in life. My old existence was almost a distant memory as I practiced stepping into the new. With renewed passion for life and the work that lay ahead, I was forever changed.

My intuitive perceptions and clarity intensified along with new opportunities for choosing. I took some time to pay attention and make a few course corrections. As I got clearer, my inner guidance got more specific. I wrote down the following good advice from the Wizard— and followed it.

Focus your time and intention on fulfilling your purpose. Everything you need will come. You will find your way by reaching for the deepest desires inside your heart. Here is where you will find the golden life and the gold in life....

Stop thinking so much about the future and begin living now. Stop holding back, and stop waiting. As you focus on the future, you must live in the present. The life you are living today is yesterday's future. But don't wait to be content and happy. You are already living the new life you have been wishing for. You are living in the present writing about finding your purpose in life and achieving Wealth Inside Out.

It is time to get your book wrapped up. You keep thinking it is a difficult long-term project. It is not. You can have this book done in a matter of weeks.... Begin weaving your personal story into the pages, but don't make such work of it.

Don't try to edit this book yourself. Find others who do this easily and let them help you. This will free you to do what you do best, which is to write and develop your work....

Let's add some story into your book right now so you can see how easy it is. Begin with a few early events that led you to finding your purpose in life.

Then in much the same way I had been writing down guidance, I began adding my story to the book. And just as the Wizard had said, in a matter of weeks most of it was written. After this, I began to think about editing.

Synchronicity

The thing always happens that you really
believe in; and the belief in a thing makes it happen.
— Frank Lloyd Wright, American architect (1867-1959)

When I first started looking for an editor, I did not know where to begin. It did not even occur to me that I needed an editor. That's how much I knew about writing a book. It was my desire to find a good technical writer who would also take a personal interest in my book. Three well-timed events occurred.

One night after our weekly yoga class, Margot Edwards, a fellow practitioner, asked Desirée and me what we had been up to. Desirée told her about our upcoming move to Hawaii, and then I casually mentioned my work in progress, which at the time was titled *The Power of Guided Purpose*. Almost immediately Margot blurted out, "I want to help edit that book." Margot told me that she enjoyed writing and used to edit medical journals. She could not explain why, but she felt compelled to help.

I met several times with Margot as she sifted tediously through the initial chapters of my first rendition and then coached me on how to refine my writing skills. Although it was not my primary goal to become a great writer, I wanted to deliver my message effectively. Margot was an enormous support; and she helped me set the tone for the entire book. But I still had a long way to go, and I needed help for the long haul.

Several months before, when Desirée and I returned from Oklahoma City after our buffalo experience, I had called Tonja Grothe, an editor in Minnesota who was introduced through a friend of a friend. After a great conversation, I had a good feeling about working with her. It was now five months later, and I was sending Tonja my revised, though preliminary, draft.

The next day, I received a remarkable e-mail from Tonja:

```
Signs Schmigns!!!! I HAD to send these!!
```

What she sent were pictures of her family sitting in front of a buffalo statue in Oklahoma City. About three months after Desirée's and my trip there, she had her first chance ever to go into downtown Oklahoma City. I was floored. The buffalo statue in the picture was the very first one Desirée and I had seen there at the botanical gardens.

That night I could not stop thinking about the buffalo. Later I dreamed of running through the streets in Oklahoma City while looking at all the buffalo statues. The next day, I got another e-mail from Tonja.

```
I've had such a connection with what I have
read so far. I was in tears most of yesterday
because it so resonated with where I am in my
life!
```

When we talked, Tonja explained that she does not normally get emotionally involved when editing. She just edits. But *Wealth Inside Out* had evoked a new process for her, and she was unable to keep from being pulled into the story. Then she told me that she felt compelled to be involved with the book.

Now the real work began as Tonja and I spent many hours delving into the next layers of the editing process. My health was getting better, and over the next three months I hung out at the computer for longer periods.

So there it was again—synchronicity, that "cubic centimeter of chance." The organizing principles of life were bringing me closer to fulfilling my purpose and achieving Wealth Inside Out.

Working with Tonja, I put together most of a manuscript. Now we needed some fresh eyes to take it to the next level. I had interviewed a couple of editors and was ready to work with one of them. The Wizard had a different plan. A few days later, I was in a boutique looking at purses for Desirée when the sales manager and I struck up a casual conversation about my book. Excited, she referred me to Ann West, who had worked on hundreds of books. As I was about to give the go-ahead to the other editor, I began hearing those familiar whispers in the night.

Work with Ann West. She is the one who can help you.

Not yet convinced, I said. "Yes, but I've already decided on another. And I was planning to call her tomorrow."

But the Wizard said again and again,

Work with Ann West. She is the one who can help you.

Since my message is about following inner guidance, I thought it wise to take my own advice. Synchronicity had delivered three different editors, each contributing valuable feedback to help me clarify my message. This was a good sign that I was on the right track.

Take a moment now to consider the synchronistic events from your life? Have you ever pursued a goal and discovered that resources suddenly appeared? What do you think your life would be like if this would happen more often?

Coming Home to Me

Unlike grownups, children have little need to deceive themselves.
— Johann Wolfgang von Goethe, German poet (1739-1832)

I did not start out on this true wealth journey with the objective of finding my purpose. I just wanted to feel excited about my direction rather than merely striving and paying bills. It's funny how life has its own way of guiding us forward. Along this journey to Wealth Inside Out I discovered so many interesting surprises.

> Often during choosing, we bump up against the very negativity and limitations that have stopped us in the past. This is normal. Rather than avoid these negative voices or pretend they don't exist, be present with them to free yourself from their grip.

For example, as my confidence grew stronger, my need for the approval of others became less important. My social encoding no longer held me back; I was choosing a new path of true wealth creation that was also choosing me.

While writing about the experience, it truly hit home how profoundly my insecurities had been affecting my decisions. With this realization, I could feel the exhaustion leaving my body. I finally got it. The freedom sought by the spirit does not come from trying to please others. After years of seeking, I was near what I wanted most—simply to feel free. I had to go lie down to let this sink in.

The Wizard encouraged me again, and I took it all to heart:

You have spent many years seeing yourself as too small, Mark, rather than as the valuable person you are by nature. The way you see yourself is what filters the wealth creation opportunities you will notice. And the way you see yourself is largely responsible for the outcomes in your life.

Suddenly, Sneaky Pete rose up in the most volatile protest ever, saying every negative thing he could think of.

"This is a dumb book," he chided. "What makes you think anyone will want to read your story? Where did you ever come up with that Wizard baloney? I can see the headlines now, 'Carmel Man Talks to the Universe.' And all this purpose stuff…there is no purpose to life. You live, and then you die. Whatever gave you the idea of some greater saintly purpose? Just do what you have to do and get busy with it…."

Negative self-talk is crippling, and I'm not sure if anyone escapes it completely, not even those who are most positive and successful. It was painful for me to hear Sneaky Pete's comments, but I have included them because they hold a valuable lesson. You can see that I still had days when I was unable to hold onto my true wealth vision. Your Sneaky Pete equivalent may also be trying to destroy your dreams. Nevertheless, all successful people have found effective ways to make the dreams of the heart bigger than their negative voices.

Often during choosing, we bump up against the very negativity and limitations that have stopped us in the past. This is normal. Rather than avoid these negative voices or pretend they don't exist, be present with them to free yourself from their grip. You may want to think of such moments as a new opportunity for unwanted patterns to peel away as you keep letting go and moving toward your goals and dreams. How wonderful to become more free to go after the true wealth dreams of your heart. This may also a good time to find the help of an expert mentor who will help you learn how to become successful and make the necessary internal shifts you need to achieve true success and happiness.

As you move deeper into choosing, be aware that each personal development strategy or technique you discover is effective only to the point that you are willing and ready to move beyond your limitations. Whenever you come to the place where it seems too difficult, suddenly the previous strategy or technique appears to have stopped working. But look deeper and ask the hard questions. Are you really off track or are you merely getting in your own way? How badly do you want Wealth Inside Out? Are you willing to persevere in choosing so that finding your purpose in life and true wealth creation can find its way of choosing you?

And the Wizard continued, giving me another boost.

Today, see yourself as big and expansive, confident and successful. Notice when you are in touch with unlimited possibilities. As your fears arise, continue letting go as you release them from your body. Then shift your focus to clear knowing and to trusting in your destiny. Keep your true wealth vision on the real you.

Keep letting go as you do what you love and follow your dreams. Keep asking for inner guidance and clarity. Get the help you need to move forward. Keep open to the many ways your purpose can manifest.

As I contemplated these words, I was reminded of the three C's — clarity, congruence and confidence. Again, I had the choice where to direct my attention. Now it was almost second nature for me to expand as I was coming home to me.

The Three C's

The three C's are primary factors that affect your true wealth outcomes. Clarity is knowing what you want. Congruence is being in sync with your vision. Confidence is being at ease with your life.

▶ *Clarity*

Clarity is most vital. Without clarity, it is difficult to take effective action toward any goal, much less to live your passion. Although clarity for me was slow in coming, my persistence and patience paid off. You may recall that at first, my only real clarity was wanting to find clarity about my true wealth direction.

In his inspirational classic *Think and Grow Rich*, Napoleon Hill (1937) suggested that lack of clarity is the number one reason for failure. He came to this remarkable conclusion after studying 500 of the most influential people of his day, people such as Henry Ford, Theodore Roosevelt, Charles Schwab, Woodrow Wilson, Thomas Edison and Alexander Graham Bell, to name a few.

As I came to finding clarity for myself, I looked at four areas: clarity as it applies to purpose, direction, focus (or goals) and values.

Clarity of purpose has to do with what you want your life to be about. It is about knowing your primary life mission. When you know your purpose in life, you can more easily find clear direction and bring forth your true wealth dreams.

Clarity of direction is about how you express your purpose. For example, if your purpose is to help others create more fulfilling relationships, your true wealth direction may be to write relationship books, or teach relationship classes, or work with married couples, or assist parents with kids, and so on. My life purpose is about helping others find theirs, and now my true wealth direction includes writing, teaching, mentoring, holding retreats and speaking. What are the ways you can begin to fulfill your purpose? Don't worry if you are not yet completely clear. Begin writing down some of your ideas that make you feel excited.

Clarity of focus includes long-range goals and where you place your focus at any given time. If you are not yet clear about your purpose or your true wealth direction, a good first goal is simply finding your purpose in life or getting clear on your direction. If you keep with the process of inner guidance and the Six Dimensions of Wealth Creation, clarity will come.

Clarity of values has to do with the principles or standards by which you live. Values represent what is important to you. Your purpose and everything you do must be in sync with your values. Otherwise you will more easily go off course. For example, if you want to go into a business but do not truly endorse your product or service, you will feel out of step. This happened with Desirée and me on several occasions as we explored many potential businesses. When considering your values, think about the nonnegotiable principles or standards you hold (or plan to hold from this point forward).

In thinking about clarity in the four areas of purpose, direction, goals and values, look beyond your current circumstances and past disappointments as a measure of your progress. Now you can begin anew with fresh clarity.

Look again at what is truly calling you? What do you most desire? This is what you will lead you to clarity. Don't worry whether you believe you can have it or not at first. Just begin to let your authentic dreams come to the surface as real possibilities.

▶ Congruence

Alignment between your true wealth vision and a well-suited outer expression is pivotal to deep fulfillment. Sure, you can learn to generate fulfillment within any circumstance, but when you fail to step toward your true wealth direction a part of you still wonders what your life would be like doing what you really love. Much like our lungs breathe air and our heart pumps blood, our dreams seek expression—automatically.

We can understand that actions of the heart and lungs are involuntary, yet we tend to think of our dreams as voluntary. That is, we have choice. But if you want to experience true success and happiness, you must allow your dreams to find their natural expression. Where you get to choose is whether to *pursue* your dreams or not. This is voluntary. Stepping toward your dreams with clarity and confidence is what brings forth a feeling of congruence.

As my core passionate stirrings to write and lead retreat programs started to find expression, *that* is when I began to find congruence. With each step I took toward my true wealth vision, I gained greater clarity, and the congruence became even more real. I needed only to expand my confidence as I continued stepping toward my passions and Wealth Inside Out.

▶ *Confidence*

> It is worth doing the inner work necessary for high self-esteem. Then you will have the real inner confidence to achieve all of your true wealth dreams.

Your confidence is so vital to realizing your purpose and achieving Wealth Inside Out that it may actually determine your success. Consider four areas of confidence: self-confidence, knowledge, skills or abilities and direction.

Self-confidence has to do with knowing your own value and your natural place in the scheme of life. Others may have their opinions, but where is your best fit now and what is your inherent value according to your own standards?

Some people are able to acknowledge their own value more easily than others can. And what a wonderful starting place if you are one who does this naturally. For those who have difficulty, I recommend you continue vigorously with the clearing process while stepping toward your true wealth vision and goals. Get whatever help you need. You will begin seeing the real you. You may even consider working with one of our Wealth Creation Mentors, one-on-one over the phone so we can help you eliminate whatever negative beliefs are holding you back from total self-confidence.

With greater self-confidence, I began seeing myself as a leader in the work of human purpose and wealth creation. I had a new foundation for living my purpose and achieving Wealth Inside Out. Are you ready for this in your life?

My knowledge confidence came as Desirée and I learned more about the nuts and bolts of our new mentoring and retreat business, such as how to start it, how to fund it, how to market it and how to run it.

Our skills and abilities confidence would come only after we had actual experience operating our new business. You can learn about something, read about it and talk about it, but until you actually do it, you will not have full understanding. That is why education, training and especially mentoring are important. Remember to work with true experts who can actually help you get clear and make the changes you need to become successful.

Our direction confidence became ever clearer with each passing day. Many of the seeming obstacles we had encountered were now behind us. By following the wisdom of intuitive clarity, Desirée and I were continually led to the best resources that would make our business successful.

Each step we took increased our confidence. We began mastering new skills in writing, speaking, working with clients and building a business. This further increased our confidence in all areas, which in turn led us to even greater clarity and focus.

With clarity of purpose and a committed direction, you can begin building your skills and abilities around your knowledge. It is worth doing the inner work necessary for high self-esteem. When you put your inner confidence behind your knowledge and skills to fulfill your true wealth calling, you bring forth congruence—a winning combination for Wealth Inside Out.

As you continue choosing the three C's and stepping toward your dreams, life will choose with you. Now you come out from the void to fulfill your purpose of true success and happiness.

Darren's Story

Darren came to me several years ago looking to create a new construction and remodeling company. This was his big dream, to become a successful building contractor. I could see that he had the passion, but he had almost no practical experience in the field. I worked with Darren to help him shape his vision and provide some time-saving tips as well. Mostly, Darren wanted to have the confidence to move forward with his dream.

After a few sessions, off he went and began choosing his true wealth vision. Within a few short years Darren was grossing over a million dollars per year. That's pretty phenomenal considering that 85% of all businesses never reach the million dollar level. Through his work with us, Darren became clear, and he had learned how to harness that clarity and turn it into wealth.

Choosing

Points to Remember

- Notice if what you are choosing is also choosing you.

- Keep moving toward your true wealth vision in whatever ways you can.

- Know that following your intuitive whispers is not always logical, and the actions you take do not always lead you where you think you are going.

- Rather than a rigid commitment of will, allow choosing to emerge from within. Focus on what you are seeking to "join together."

- Don't wait for your fear to go away to begin taking action. Choose one piece of intuitive clarity you are willing to act upon, and then take even one small step forward.

- Pay attention to synchronicity and what flows naturally.

- Keep asking for clarity everyday, saying the words "What's my purpose?" "What is my next step?" and the like.

- Don't get bogged down over which inner messages are literal and which are symbolic. As you follow the callings of your heart, enjoy the exploration and see where they lead.

- Come out of the void as you leave the old behind while moving toward the new.

- The way you see yourself determines what actions you will take. Stop holding back and let the real you come forth.

- Ask yourself the hard questions. Are you really off track, or are you merely getting in your own way? How sincerely do you want to realize your true wealth goals and achieve Wealth Inside Out?

- Watch out for negative voices that may rise to the surface during choosing. Don't let them throw you off.

- Pay attention to the 3 C's—clarity, congruence and confidence. Build upon each of them to reinforce the others, thereby providing a winning combination for true success and happiness.

For more powerful exercises about choosing that will help you achieve wealth from the inside out, download your supplementary *Wealth Creation Workbook* at www.WealthCreationWorkbook.com.

Chapter Eight

WEALTH INSIDE OUT

Living the Life You Love

Go confidently in the direction of your dreams.
Live the life you've imagined.
—Henry David Thoreau, American author (1817-1862)

We've learned a lot about finding your purpose and true wealth creation, and you now have an overview of this natural process. But how do you practice living a life you love? There needs to be alignment between your inner desires and ways of living. You need balance between your heart and head, between making plans and letting go. Once you are fully in touch with your deeper true wealth desires, it may become difficult to follow any other path.

This book has shared my journey. I suspended ordinary logic and stepped into the void to pass through the Six Dimensions of Wealth Creation. Perhaps my experiences will inspire your own journey to finding your purpose in life and creating Wealth Inside Out. By now you may have a clearer sense of how to find your passion and what is calling you. All that stands between you and a new way of life is laying claim to your special mission.

Following the intuitive whispers that beckon, you will unleash your inner wisdom and your renewed personal power, allowing new portals to open. Nevertheless, do not altogether dismiss your ordinary logic and deductive reasoning, for these too serve an important function. You will only need to know when to use such faculties and when to let them rest. Your logic will keep you grounded in the physical realities of life as you explore all that exists beyond the normal bounds of reasoning.

For example, my fear of following my dreams and the longings of my heart had kept me from my true wealth path. I was so focused on the security of my future that I was unable to listen to the wisdom of the present. My logic was blocking me. The loss of security finally got my attention when health and finances took a dive. It is ironic that the very goal I was striving to attain was temporarily thwarted—just long enough to cause me to shift my focus toward my passion in life and what I most wanted.

Many success programs talk about doing what you love. Others help you make plans and goals. So what is the real key? When you follow only your heart, you may find what you love, but not necessarily the way to make your life work. When you follow only your head, you may handle the practical necessities of life but get lost doing only what you *have* to do. Either way, you end up with a lack of alignment. Your heart and your head are not on the same page.

The key to Wealth Inside Out is putting your heart in front of your head and then using your head to support the dreams of your heart. Just don't get stuck in your head. It can stop you in your tracks and prevent your life's provident direction from taking hold. To live a life you love, your quest for true wealth and happiness must be a priority. Then you can move forward with focus and veracity.

As I have staked my claim in my true wealth purpose, my life has truly changed. I have reconnected with childlike wonder and with the excitement of what keeps unfolding in front of me. I love waking up each morning to new conversations with Desirée. I love my morning practices of breathing, meditation and writing down the Wizard's commentary. Sneaky Pete has become less and less influential. Through intuitive wisdom and guided clarity, I am living a life I love. So can you.

A Brief Review

You might want to review The Six Dimensions of Wealth Creation (Figure 4). Where do you find yourself now compared with when you started? Remember your journey is not always linear, so you may be traversing several dimensions simultaneously.

Figure 4

Six Dimensions of Wealth Creation

6

WEALTH INSIDE OUT

(The Sixth Dimension)
Fulfills your passions and
your purpose. Your path
leads to financial, interpersonal,
physical and spiritual wealth.

Although displayed here as a sequence, the path one may take does
not need to follow this route exactly.
In fact, beginning the quest of Wealth
Inside Out often triggers circumstances
that bring all the dimensions into play.
Notice how each dimension invokes
new layers of letting go as you move
toward your purpose.

5

CHOOSING

(The Fifth Dimension)
Commitment to new direction
revealed through inner guidance and
clear knowing. Install new beliefs that
support your true wealth vision. Trust
that life holds a definite place for you.
Come out of the void.

1

RUMBLINGS

(The First Dimension)
Inner longings, yearnings and intuitive
whispers. Deep sense of knowing of your
passions in life. You carry this knowing
with you. Become aware of what is
calling you.

2

ENDINGS

(The Second Dimension)
Realization that you can no longer continue your
current direction. Often involves upheaval or
catalytic life change. New beginning may not
yet be clear. You may enter the void.
Let go of old ways.

4

CLEARING

(The Fourth Dimension)
Eliminate old beliefs, fears and emotional
baggage and reevaluate relationships. Release
ego's need to know everything. Learn to trust
life as you harness the power of the higher
organizing principle.

3

GUIDANCE

(The Third Dimension)
Inner wisdom and intuitive hunches.
Asking for help from inner source of power, God or
universal intelligence. See new realities and new
possibilities. Let go of how you think things work.
Employ the guidance of experts.

VOID

Somewhere between endings and choosing you may come upon a journey to the void.
This is a time of incubation, gestation and recalibration. Often it elicits feelings of confusion and uncertainty
as you bridge the gap between old ways of being and finding your way to Wealth Inside Out. The void is
valuable even though it is a time in which nothing seems to be moving. Release old realities and beliefs as new
ones are forming during this time. This is *not* a good time for planning or goal setting. Allow clarity to come
first through inner guidance and clearing. This natural gestation period will do its job of bringing you
to your purpose and Wealth Inside Out.

Taking the Next Steps

When you have to make a choice and don't make it, that in itself is a choice.
— William James, American psychologist (1842-1910)

As Desirée and I began planning for our move to Hawaii, I would occasionally encounter lingering twinges of doubt. Then a phone call came from someone who asked me to build a house in Monterey. Desirée and I had gone a long time without steady income, so the thought of taking the project was tempting. Sneaky Pete was all over this little development, doing everything possible to convince me to go for it. I knew the job would delay our move to Hawaii for at least another year and a half. Fortunately, the Wizard was not at all swayed by these changes in our situation or by Sneaky Pete's misguided attempts to hold us back.

> Your inner guidance and clarity run much deeper than impulse and momentary passion. Yet it will also challenge you to move past your fears and limiting beliefs. Get the expert help you need to get unstuck and to be able follow your true wealth dreams.

Desirée and I were face to face with a choice. Would we continue toward our vision of Wealth Inside Out or cave to the old life we had left behind? Was this a test of our commitment? What would we choose?

Although fearful about the move, we were even more afraid of going backward. Neither of us could see ourselves living the life we had given up.

The next day, I canceled our appointment with the prospective home-building client. We made the choice to continue our true wealth direction. Soon after, we had the final sales contract on our apartments, which closed out successfully a couple of months later. *Wealth Inside Out* was near completion, and Desirée had begun her healing and wealth mentoring work with people. We were solidly on our path.

As you consider your own choices along the way to your true wealth purpose, be thoughtful of your unique situation. For example, just as I had sensed early on, Desirée and I would end up investing much of our money into our new direction before success grabbed hold. Many people like the *idea* of a new direction, but are not willing to do what it takes to succeed. If that is the case for you, why keep fooling yourself. Either step into it or let it go.

We do not recommend that you immediately quit your job or run off in a new direction you may not yet comprehend. The particular ways you navigate transition has much to do with your individual style and your tolerance for risk along with your financial ability. Remember that your inner guidance and clarity run much deeper than impulse and momentary passion. Clear guidance will make you more discerning and stable, not less. But it will also challenge you to move past your fears, limiting beliefs or circumstances. In contrast, denying your connection will leave you feeling out of sync. Following your innermost wisdom and clarity will set you on your true wealth path as long as you sincerely listen and take focused action to follow your dreams. Remember to get the expert help you need to get unstuck and begin moving forward.

More From the Wizard

When you do what you have to do,
You may find what you like to do,
When you do what you are called to do,
You get to do what you were born to do
—The Wizard

You see, Mark, this book serves several purposes. First, it launches you immediately into fulfilling your true wealth purpose, and the story on these pages will launch others to do the same. It also anchors you while you are writing your next book and building retreat programs.

Now, let yourself be immersed in your true wealth direction without the limitations of the past. You are well on your way. Just keep going.

Wealth Inside Out will take you leaps and bounds into whatever success you know in your heart wants to come forth. But watch out for Sneaky Pete, who will try to control your life. Let the wisdom of your inner source be your guide. This is what will lead you to true success and happiness.

Remember though, that nothing happens until you step forward. You must act with confidence upon your sincere inner knowing. Focus on the energy of true wealth creation and what wants to be expressed through you. You must make the phone call, write the book, ask for help, share your dream with others and move toward your vision as if there was no question about its success. Do not wait until you have it all together. Do not plan everything you need to say to someone. Be yourself and share from your heart. Step beyond your fear and into the passion of what you are doing. This is what inspires others toward finding Wealth Inside Out.

Just as the Wizard had promised, when I finally stopped fighting with myself, I began to shift into a more natural flow with life and become less afraid. At last, I understood that I didn't have to know how it was all going to work out in order to take action. I became free to mobilize my focus. The words for the book were pouring out of me like the waters of Niagara Falls, sometimes so fast I could barely write them down.

Ways of Blocking Wealth Inside Out

We foolishly believe that our own limitations
are the proper measure of limitations.
— Napoleon Hill, American author (1883-1970)

If you have been unable to access your true wealth vision and clarity, it usually means you are either too afraid or you are blocking, or both. Remember that it is possible to increase your capacity for intuition and clear knowing through practices that enhance mind-body-spirit integration, such as yoga, meditation, breathwork and other methods. Even making your dreams more important than your fears will help you hear all that life wants you to know.

> Be willing to receive your inner guidance even when it may not fit with your schedule.

Really, we are being led with intuitive clarity all the time. It is part of our make-up as humans. Much the as blood flows through our body, intuitive clarity flows through our being. However, you may discover at least four blocks to your inner wisdom, each of them based in some form of fear.

First, we may not *want* to know. We may be afraid to hear our innermost wisdom because we don't want to know the truth. This fear is about being responsible. Knowing the truth requires that we take responsibility, either for the way our lives have turned out or for creating the life we love.

It is often much easier to place blame on others for your circumstances or for why you can't have the life you truly want. Remember, this way of thinking will not get you where you want to go. You have to be willing to take responsibility or you will block the clarity that would otherwise help you get on track.

Second, you may have limiting beliefs. If you have been taught that the world works a certain way, you can fail to fully examine your own truth, which in turn will affect your natural guidance system. For example, if you have adopted a particular belief system, it is likely that you will block whatever wisdom does not fit within the parameters of your beliefs. This is usually due to fear of persecution but may also be about taking responsibility. You must find the courage to handle the influences that have been keeping you from expressing your truth. I am not suggesting you abandon your faith, but make sure that what you believe is real for you.

Third, you may be placing too many parameters around your request. You may be saying something such as, "Please give me guidance and clarity about my health, but just don't tell me to start exercising," or "Please give me guidance about my finances, and even though my spouse manages money far better, don't tell me to let her or him manage the money." You get the idea.

The third way of blocking has its roots in fear of loss. You want to be connected with your intuitive clarity, but only upon certain conditions — ones that do not require you to give up something. However, to receive clear, confident inner directives, you must make your requests without the burden of other agendas. Just make pure, simple, open-ended requests. You can say, "Please give me guidance about improving my relationships." Period! No *ifs, ands* or *buts.*

Fourth, you may block inner guidance by being stubborn. We often hide behind our intellectual knowledge, assuming we've already come up with the best answers. This is a fear of letting go as we work hard to control the environment.

For example, before I learned about intuitive wisdom, I used to make plans and goals that had nothing to do with being in sync with my true wealth vision. I was confident that I had the correct strategic maneuvers figured out. In reality, I had lost touch with my deepest desires. I was afraid to even hear my inside callings and especially afraid to follow them. If I stepped toward the inner whispers to go after my real dreams, would I go down a path that did not support me financially? Then there was my fear that Sneaky Pete would succeed at messing it all up. Even six months into my Wealth Inside Out transition, I was tempted to go back to my old ways.

One day Desirée made a revealing comment about how fear works against us. This rang true for me. She said, "I'm sometimes afraid to receive guidance because I fear that it will tell me to do something that doesn't fit with my schedule." That says it in a nutshell.

When we are unable to hear the wisdom within our own system, it is common to find a hidden agenda tucked away in our subconscious. It often has to do with our time, finances or with a situation we don't want to give up. However, trying to control every outcome will often block the very wisdom that would bring resolution to a situation. Sure you may be drawn to do something that at first seems daunting, but you have to keep looking at the big picture. Are you truly going in the right direction, or are you merely trying to force a particular outcome even when life is nudging you in another direction?

So how can you deal with your blocks and fears? First, remember you are not alone. Life wants you to succeed. However, you have to do your part and ask for help, even when you are afraid. Ask to be set free of your fears so they no longer stop you. Be willing to look at other options as you recalibrate. Get the help of true experts who will help you win.

Your Purpose and Relationships

It is important to look at the way our personal life transitions affect the other people in our lives, especially those closest to us. Whenever one person enters a substantial transition, others must also make changes. Sometimes the changes may go smoothly, and other times they can ruffle the feathers of our relationships. In a marriage, for example, if both partners are on the same page about the changes, transition can be relatively smooth. However, when one person enters a transition, and the other wants to keep things the same, there will be issues to wade through. Because Desirée and I were committed to each other's changes, we took in stride the upheaval caused by our Wealth Inside Out journey.

If you and your significant other are not in agreement, I suggest you each find a place of loving cooperation and respect while moving toward your respective visions and goals. Can you love your mate and yourself at the same time?

Probably the most helpful tool is to stay connected with your heart as you strengthen your inner power. What does your highest wisdom keep telling you? You have to trust that you can handle your relationships with integrity and without compromising your values and clarity. Keep in mind that although people close to you might initially resist changes, they will also come around to support you when they sense your new direction taking hold. Remember, your higher self always knows what to do.

Don't Give Up

One of the most common causes of failure is the habit of quitting when one is overtaken by temporary defeat.
—Napoleon Hill, American author (1883-1970)

There may be times when you feel pulled to give up on your true wealth dreams. In fact, your Sneaky Pete may be working to throw you off track. If you made it this far in the book, many openings are occurring simultaneously—spiritually, psychologically and emotionally. You may even feel like an exposed nerve as you explore new frontiers. Although the side effects of finding your compass may be uncomfortable, they signal that you've moved closer to completing your Wealth Inside Out transition. Keep following the callings of your heart and the wisdom of your inner knowing.

The deeper you reach into the core of who you are, the more aligned you become with your destiny. Allow yourself to be genuinely receptive to the messages life is trying to reveal. As you follow your inner whispers, trust the natural process of life to reorganize around your true wealth vision and around what you were born to do. In the next chapter, Desirée emphasizes that what you truly value is held within your purpose.

Whatever you do, don't give up. Think of times when you and others have triumphed. Think of sports and how many games are won in the final moments. Following your dreams is an even greater game, one that pulsates with meaning and fulfillment, true success and happiness. There is nothing else like it. Get whatever support you need and keep choosing. Keep letting go and keep going.

Variations on Living Your Purpose

Noble purpose is not always a call to the extraordinary. More often than not it is the embrace of the ordinary, some basic urge or impulse that makes you feel simply satisfied and good.
— Barry Heermann, American author

When finding your purpose in life, you may be looking for something lofty or noble. But don't get stuck thinking higher purpose has to be extraordinary. Your purpose is mostly about what has personal meaning to you and what makes your heart sing. In his book, *Noble Purpose*, Barry Heermann (2004) poses this as any way you feel called to serve. Purpose is about "igniting extraordinary passion" for whatever you want to express. Your purpose can be as simple as being a loving parent or an inspiration to others.

You may also find purpose in everyday matters. For example, my primary purpose is to help others discover how to become successful, find their purposes in life, create wealth and achieve their dreams, but I also have the purpose of being a good husband for Desirée and a good friend to those close to me. All of us have the purpose of taking care of our basic necessities such as our health, finances and family.

What differentiates your primary purpose or your true wealth purpose from all others is that it will feel like a definite calling. It is what you know deep down that you came here to do. What do you simply *have* to do? What do you want your life to be about? What feeds you most deeply?

The following are examples of the primary purpose of some well-known people in their own words.

- Mother Teresa: To care for and comfort the poor, sick and needy all over the world.

- Walt Disney: To make people happy.

- Henry Ford: To mass produce, mass distribute and mass consume automobiles.

- Robert Kiyosaki: To elevate the financial well-being of humanity.

Your purpose may include similar themes, such as

- To bring beauty into the world

- To move and inspire others

- To make people laugh

- To help others heal

- To help resolve conflict

- To build community

- To help people communicate effectively

- To help businesses grow

- To encourage responsible growth and development

- To protect and to serve

- To be a great mother or father

The list is endless.

It is not necessary to think too much about finding your purpose in life. When you ask for help, your inner guides speak to you. Say the words out loud "What's my purpose?" then listen carefully to what comes through. Write down your inner whispers, allowing them to keep coming until they begin to make sense.

In *Think and Grow Rich*, Napoleon Hill identified purpose as a "calling for which you are suited." (p.29) When people who have handled their fears begin to move toward their definite major purpose, the methods and resources for achieving it will appear along the way. So it is important to take that first step. Trust that what you are to do at each new crossroad will become increasingly clear.

Sharing many timeless principles, Hill talks about how success often begins in the midst of crisis. Here is where we meet our "other selves." Although *Think and Grow Rich* was written in 1937, its fundamental principles are similar to the best advice offered today. Hill begins with the topic "definiteness of purpose" to describe the essential qualities of a winner. Not only did he find that lack of clarity was the number one reason for failure among people he studied, but he identified that being

> It is important to take that first step and trust that what you do at each new crossroad will become clear.

clear about what one wants as the number one quality in creating true success and happiness. His book is not as much about money as it is about the fundamental traits of creating success and going after the dreams of your heart. This is where Desirée and I got off track, by putting our financial goals ahead of what we most wanted. Now we were putting these in right order.

Take a moment right now to reflect upon your most important priorities. Are you doing for money what you love? Do you feel connected with your passions and fulfilling your sense of purpose? Do your relationships fill you up? Are you putting your true wealth goals in the right order?

Inner Purpose — Outer Purpose

*In this age, when technology has advanced, we have cared
very little for the emotional and spiritual needs of people.*
— Sri Sri Ravi Shankar, Indian spiritual master (1956-)

When I began hiking the Appalachian Trail in the spring of 1984, I made two decisions. First, I was going to complete the entire journey from start to finish, and second, I would keep my spirits up no matter how uncomfortable I became. The first decision was about my outer journey, the second about the inner. One was about what I was *doing*, the other about how I was *being*. No matter what the focus, we all face these same choices. How are we being with what we are doing?

When you do what you love, it is easier to keep up your spirits. In fact, this is often the very activity that will lift you. It is also a good measure of whether you are on track or not. Simply observe the way you are *being* with your day-to-day journey. If what you are doing does not lift you, chances are you are not in sync with your true wealth vision. Perhaps your "ordinary logic" is pulling you off course.

Inner purpose is about being present with your moment-to-moment journey as you go about fulfilling outer purpose. Outer purpose is the mission you feel called to express in the world. One is about where you are headed and the other is about your internal state of being. Rather than looking solely to your outer purpose for fulfillment, you can bring internal satisfaction to the work of your true wealth vision.

For example, there are many daily tasks that must be completed to keep our wealth mentoring and retreat programs running smoothly. Sometimes we are growing faster than we can delegate the tasks involved. Desirée and I may end up handling too many aspects of our business. This is when we get the opportunity to practice our skills of the inner journey—being present with what is happening in the outer. Regardless of how much you love what you are doing, the outer journey will require you to keep reaching for greater attunement of the inner.

Goals and Wealth Inside Out

The saddest places on earth are graveyards. Not because people are buried there, but because dreams, talents, and purposes that never came to fruition are buried there. Graveyards are filled with books that were never written, songs that were never sung, words that were never spoken, things that were never done.
— Mark Victor Hansen, American motivational speaker,
trainer and coauthor of *Chicken Soup for the Soul* (1948-)

Once you are certain of your true wealth direction, making plans and setting goals come with remarkable clarity. Putting your life on track with purpose gives you the advantage of co-creating with the infinite. It becomes hard to fail. But you need to balance willfulness with the wisdom of your inner power to stay on course. True success gives you an enormous boost in confidence, but don't get your ego confused with your inner source. Remember who you are and how you got where you are. Never lose that.

It is important to understand that your goals are not your purpose, and neither is your job. Goals are what you aim to accomplish, and your job is what you do for a living. Purpose is about what you feel called to express in the world. You may find this through your goals or the job you do, but your true wealth purpose is found only deep within your fundamental nature. You have special gifts and talents that no one else brings to the matrix of life in quite the same way. It is mind-boggling when you think about it.

Make sure your goals are in alignment with your true wealth direction and that they fulfill your passions and all that you love in life. Going after goals that do not support what you love in life will only wear you down and take you off your path.

Until the time when Desirée and I began helping others to create wealth, I had never thought of myself as any kind of expert on the topic of money, even though we had done well financially. My strong suit has always been in what makes people tick. Why do we do the things we do? What are the *inner* dynamics that allow some people to become more successful?

When we first began moving in our own Wealth Inside Out direction, helping people build this bridge between their inner dynamics and wealth creation was not even on our radar screen (at least not consciously) much less a goal. It was through the journey of inner guidance and seeking the guidance of experts that our talents for helping others create wealth came into focus.

As Desirée and I traveled the seminar circuits, we became curious about why some people found success, but most did not. Even with good information and viable strategies, many students would not follow through or apply what they had learned.

We recognized an enormous need. Only a very small percentage of seminar students *ever* apply the knowledge and make any money. In fact, many people lose money by going to more and more seminars. This is not usually because the programs are bad; most of them are quite good and the trainers are excellent. So what is the missing link?

Sadly we saw so many people pursuing financial dreams, but without clear direction and without realizing the internal requirements of success. Pursuing money without passion rarely works (at least not for long). And you cannot succeed without having the right inner dynamics for what you are doing.

How did we go from being $70,000 in debt to making our first million dollars in less than three years? I can tell you this. Knowledge and hard work alone are not enough. I know many people with more knowledge than we have and who are willing to work harder than we do, but who are not more successful. Desirée and I have uncovered the most vital factors that determine your success and happiness.

The first vital factor is that you need a clear direction. Most people do not know how to get focused on the right course for their most important priorities. That is one of the reasons I have written this book—to help you identify your passions and get focused on them. How can you create wealth *and* do what you love?

The second vital factor for creating Wealth Inside Out is that you must be willing to make the changes that are necessary to reach success. You cannot succeed at anything until you have the right thoughts and beliefs for your specific objectives. Most people don't realize the power of their hidden inner conversations, yet they affect your wealth creation abilities in every way including your relationships, health, financial wellbeing and your happiness.

When Desirée and I were in construction and investing in real estate, we learned how to cultivate the right dynamics for success. Whenever we felt stuck, we went to expert mentors who helped us eliminate the limiting beliefs that had held us back. You can take all the trainings in the world on a topic, but success comes only when you have the right inner dynamics for what you are doing.

The third vital factor for success is having the right support system. One of the most sobering discoveries that Desirée and I have made is that often after a few months of completing a seminar or immersion program, people have the tendency to go back to old ways of living and slowly forget about their new capabilities. Transforming your life will take commitment.

Often the only missing ingredient for people who struggle to maintain what they have learned is a powerful support system. When I was deep in debt and starting over, I trained with one of my mentors every single week for more than a year so I could reprogram my mind for success. Reading books and going to seminars is a great starting point, but all the successful people I know have a phenomenal support system. That is how you achieve your goals and Wealth Inside Out.

You can learn much more about the vital factors that determine your wealth creation success. Download the free special report from our Website titled "The Seven Biggest Mistakes Most Wealth Seekers

Make and How You Can Avoid Them." Again, this download is free at
www.SpecialWealthReport.com.

Anything Is Possible

You are never given a dream without also
being given the power to make it true.
— Richard Bach, American novelist (1936-)

The choices you see for yourself may too often fall into a narrow range
that is predetermined by your beliefs. You might look at your current
situation and think the options you have already explored are the only
ones. However, there are always more options than the ones in front
of you. When you set out to discover your purpose and Wealth Inside
Out, try blowing the lid off whatever possibilities you currently are
able to comprehend.

A good way to begin is by holding the idea that anything is possible.
Anything! Consider that some new possibility exists for whatever
constrains you. A simple shift in attitude alone could expand any
limitation. Whatever your circumstances may be, think of at least one
other person who overcame even worse ones. How did they persevere
and succeed? When we are open, we begin to view things differently.
Almost like magic, we discover new options.

Many people fail to realize that purpose will express itself naturally
by unlocking from their habitual, patterned responses. Imagine what
you could achieve if you were never subjected to the limitations imposed
by your encoded beliefs. With them out of the way, your purpose and
true wealth creation have no other choice but to express. You naturally
move forward without such concern about all that could go wrong.
Not that you should be unaware of possible harms, but only as a means
for keeping on course. Your primary focus should be on what will go
right.

Life works like a beautiful flower. A seed is planted; it absorbs water
and sunlight as well as nutrients from the soil, and voila! The seed that
is already within blossoms. Now imagine covering a flower so that no
air, light or water can reach it. The flower would die. Negative thoughts
and beliefs work much the same way to cover your natural expression.

The mask of unwanted programs destroys possibilities and shuts down your inherent expression of purpose and Wealth Inside Out.

Give your dreams the air and light and nourishment of believing in yourself. When you move toward the true wealth callings of your heart, your inherent expression can't help but happen. Focus on the thoughts and beliefs you *need* to be successful with your dreams. Opportunities will open beyond what you can imagine.

> To know and live your true wealth purpose brings you the kind of success and happiness that most people only dream about.

Now you can get yourself busy talking to people as you allow your dreams to unfold naturally and easily. Don't worry so much about what forms they take. These will become clear as you begin sharing your true wealth vision with others. Refuse to let yourself worry. Say "no" to unrewarding thoughts and belief patterns that bring you down. Keep believing in your dreams and how you will bring them into reality. Write down your thoughts of clear knowing and look at them every day.

Give yourself the freedom to explore. Read books and attend retreats or seminar programs; step out of your box. Consider new ideas that stretch the bounds of ordinary logic. You will uncover fresh insights and renewed inspiration. Be persistent about finding your true wealth purpose. There is no deeper satisfaction than knowing your purpose and expressing it in the world. This is the awesome power of Wealth Inside Out.

Observe your inner voices. Who is speaking to you? Do you follow your Sneaky Pete or your Wizard? As you follow your true wealth dreams and the callings of your heart, will you play out the unconscious patterns of your past or remember who you really are and achieve Wealth Inside Out? Whenever you feel unsure, remember that anything is possible.

On Your Way

It is difficult, at first, for most people to follow guidance.
In the beginning, it requires a bit of blind faith and trust.
— The Wizard

All of my experiences with inner guidance and the journey on which it has taken me have opened many new doors. At first I simply had to surrender. Then I looked for ways to focus my efforts effectively. I had to learn the delicate dance between effort and surrender. As I got on board with my true wealth vision, balance for life came more easily. Writing this book, for example, came effortlessly, yet I've never worked harder at anything in my life. I put in long hours, but I was energized by my efforts. I was so inspired about getting out such a powerful message that I sometimes forgot how much I was working.

I also gained renewed trust in the organizing principles of life—the intelligence that communicates what to do next through intuition and synchronistic events. Whether this sense of knowing is found through your faith, through your thoughts and feelings or from intuition, everybody has access to the benevolent resources of the infinite. It is not a gift reserved for a chosen few. It is everyone's birthright.

Whatever obstacles you face in opening to clarity, always remember the rewards are worth the price. As you follow your true wealth knowing and put aside whatever limitations have kept you stuck, your life will begin to work in a new, sometimes unimaginable way.

Don't wait for proof about how these principles work. That will only get in your way. Do exactly the opposite. You must first open yourself to hear your intuitive wisdom, and place confidence in this innate process of life and trust that you will naturally reorganize around your true wealth priorities. Believe me, I was disappointed at not having proof beforehand. But you cannot plan the guidance that is naturally running through you. There are no guarantees in life. However, when you are receptive your intuitive wisdom will be there for you in some way. If nothing comes in the beginning, go back again to clearing. Continue reviewing the Six Dimensions of Wealth Creation until your true wealth vision comes forth.

You have to engage the process for it to work. You may also need to let go of rigid agendas. It may seem backward and defy your ordinary logic, yet taking these actions will open the way to your true success and happiness. In time, you will build a track record of new experiences that will eventually become the proof that you have been looking for. The initial steps require a bit of blind faith—maybe even a lot. You will need to make the first moves and remain open, perhaps even diligent. If things still do not open, a part of you is blocking further progress. You may have to dig deeper. Remember to get the help you need.

Watch out for your Sneaky Pete. He will try to run your life if you do not intervene on your own behalf. Find your wise inner voice. He (or she) is millions of times more powerful than Sneaky Pete, but *you* are the one who must choose what voice to follow.

Don't wait for everything to *make sense*. Simply start moving toward your true wealth vision and what is calling you. Keep in mind that if your ordinary logic had already taken you where you *really* wanted to go, it is unlikely you would be wondering what to do. You may also find it helpful to attend one of our Wealth Inside Out training programs, where you will learn specialized wealth creation skills and get the support you need to be successful.

Remember that what actually opens may be different than what you have focused on. So be ready for some exciting surprises. I was initially so focused on the retreat center vision that I was resistant to the idea of writing a book. But once I started to follow the intuitive callings of *write books, write books, write books*, I became unstoppable. I didn't try to make it happen. It expressed through me naturally. Now I cannot imagine my life without this book.

To know and live your true wealth purpose brings you the kind of success and happiness that most people only dream about. Your purpose is there, always looking for a way to express itself. You need only to commit to knowing what it is and then get busy living it.

Raymond's Story

For a long time, Raymond had been going to various seminars on how to create wealth. He had read dozens of books on real estate and thought that would make him rich. And while he had learned a lot of facts, he was not able to integrate that knowledge until he came to me for help. Prior to our program, Raymond said he felt like a hamster in a wheel, going from one seminar program to another and from one business idea to the next, running here and there. He was not successful because he was listening to what had worked for the speakers and did not know what would work for him based upon his *own* true wealth passions and upon finding the best wealth creation fit or his unique personality and values.

Desirée and I helped Raymond to identify his true passions and find the best fit. We helped him overcome his blind spots and the blind spots of others to clearly see his true wealth opportunities. Next we helped him develop his own unique approach to real estate. A short time later, Raymond was finally able to land his first real estate deal, and he made over $500,000 in less than two years.

Many people are just like Raymond. They mistakenly think that the only knowledge they need is knowledge of investments, or knowledge of real estate, or knowledge of the stock market. While that knowledge is very important, it is not sufficient to enable you to become wealthy in that field. You have to combine it with the power of self-knowledge and be willing to make the changes that are necessary to achieve success.

When you discover your true wealth purpose and focus on your most important dreams, you open the gateway that allows you to harness your passions and turn them into wealth. That is when you will finally achieve wealth from the inside out.

Kamuela Life Retreats and
Wealth Inside Out Trainings

What a different story men would have to tell if only they would adopt a definite purpose, and stand by that purpose until it had time to become an all-consuming obsession!
— Napoleon Hill, American author (1883-1970)

Following ordinary logic, Desirée and I started out with *goals* to build wealth through real estate. We had *plans* to grow our construction business. Now we live our true wealth passions, helping others find theirs. Sure we still have plans and goals, but they are in alignment with our purpose and what we most value. We even use logic as an important tool. But the new inner filters through which we sift our thoughts have expanded our view of what is possible. We had to shelve ordinary logic for a while to get on our true wealth path and discover Wealth Inside Out.

Through the journey of finding our purposes in life, the vision Desirée and I have for a retreat center is being expressed by using the seminar venues of others. The original business vision of Kamuela Holistic Resort has become Kamuela Life Retreats and Wealth Inside Out Trainings. Our programs now include a wide variety of wealth creation skills and strategies that anyone can learn and use to find true success and happiness. You can find out more about these programs by visiting our Website at www.WealthInsideOut.com.

You may not need to write a book or find a buffalo to achieve your true wealth dreams. However, if you want to create Wealth Inside Out in your life, you do need to find *your* compass and learn to follow it. Only then will you find your deepest callings and what you were born to do.

Everyone has a dream inside that wants to happen. And you can have your dream—as long as you are willing to learn and do what it takes to have it. If you are not clear about what to do, simply ask for guidance—and listen.

Wealth Inside Out

Points to Remember

- Don't let this book be just another interesting story. All that stands between you and you own Wealth Inside Out is staking your claim.

- Know when to use your ordinary logic and when to let it rest. Do not let your mind block you from your true wealth wisdom and clarity.

- Don't give up. Think of times you have triumphed. Find your internal compass for your true wealth direction. If you have not been able to access your internal guidance mechanism, remember to make your dreams more important than your fears.

- Don't get stuck thinking that your purpose has to be lofty or noble. It is primarily about what you feel called to do and what makes your heart sing.

- Your goals are not your purpose. Goals are what you *aim* to accomplish. Purpose is about what you *feel called* to express in the world. Make sure your goals are congruent with your true wealth purpose and all that you love.

- Purpose and true wealth creation naturally seek expression when you unlock yourself from the programming that has kept you stuck.

- Remember the difference between inner purpose and outer purpose. The inner is about your state of mind and your personal growth. The outer is about what you express in the world. Focus on your inner happiness and winning as you go about achieving your true wealth dreams.

- Along with your true wealth purpose, find purpose in everyday matters such as taking care of loved ones or whatever brings you joy.

- Always play the game of anything is possible. Then you have new choices for creating a life you love.

- Step forward into your true wealth vision and begin living your big dream. When you are not sure what to do, ask for guidance— and listen.

For more powerful exercises that will help you achieve wealth from the inside out, download your supplementary *Wealth Creation Workbook* at www.WealthCreationWorkbook.com.

You are not here merely to make a living. You are here to enable the world more amply, with greater vision, with a finer spirit of hope and achievement. You are here to enrich the world, and you impoverish yourself if you forget the errand.
—Woodrow Wilson, American president (1856-1924)

Chapter Nine

REFLECTIONS by DESIRÉE

What the heart knows today,
the head will understand tomorrow.
—James Stephens, Irish poet (1882-1950)

When I found myself in the middle of the biggest spiritual transformation of my life, I felt grateful. My connection to divine guidance consumed me in the softness of surrender. I finally let go to something other than my carefully constructed identity, a false identity that was slowly stripped away. I saw it as the *protective* mask it was. I could stand naked now, hands outstretched to the heavens and ready to receive what life held for me and to give what life expected of me. My spirit was demanding more from life. I experienced a test of faith that, in the past, I could only imagine was reserved for the noble, the pure, the mystics and saints of lore—not for an average woman like me, living an ordinary life.

I was also grateful because even amid the chaos and uncertainty that I was experiencing, I had never felt more alive and more in love with life. Something awakened in me, and a very deep and exquisite kind of healing occurred. Self-doubt was not as important as my desire to find my purpose in life and to experience this wealth from the inside out amplified. I examined each of my closely held beliefs, many of which I had adopted from others and from my culture. Then using the powerful processes we have learned and developed, I discarded those beliefs that no longer held truth for me. My beliefs about being a woman, being married and being human were all up for reevaluation. I became unwilling to blindly follow the ways of the masses any longer, not without examination and my own clear direction. Some beliefs I have suspended until further notice.

I was grateful, too, because my husband Mark was finally content with his direction. I hadn't seen him this happy since we fell in love.

His heart was now coupled with his head, and he was once again reconnected to his interior. He was healing and transforming before my eyes. His passion for life returned, and our relationship became infinitely more intimate as we each went through a new individuation process.

There is freedom, I discovered, in being authentically me and expressing from my heart's desire. When the masks are removed, the paradox is apparent; we are all so much the same, yet so individually unique. We are all artists of life, and being heart-connected gives us a grounded focus to create the most fulfilling expressions.

Mark and I were doing what we had learned to do growing up and by studying the success of others. We planned, we set goals, we worked hard. We searched for our wealth-building niche, desperately at times. We tried to stay ahead in a game that our financial gurus thought would bring us security and freedom. And we were plowing forward regardless of the costs. Taking charge of our financial future was an important goal, which we believe is responsible and necessary in our uncertain times. But what we failed to understand was the importance of being heart-connected with our path toward wealth creation.

Now, I am redirecting my life around the desires of my own heart. Instead of making plans, I first ask for inner guidance and clarity. I look to see that my internal visions and rumblings are in alignment with the whispers of my heart and I then do what it says. I have reflected upon important questions such as: What do I love to do? What is my purpose in life? What unique gifts and talents do I have to give? How can I create true wealth that makes a difference?

> Play the game of anything is possible as you focus on your true wealth vision. Then go create the life of your dreams.

On that sunny morning in July 2004 when Mark and I played the game of anything is possible, we felt full of energy and confident we could do anything. We both loved the vision of a retreat center and were very excited by this idea.

When I first fell in love with Mark and we were starting to create a life together, I already had the sense that we would be working together helping people with their lives. Then the years passed with both of us choosing to make our living in construction and real-estate investing. We both knew this direction was not our purpose, but it paid the bills very well. During those years of attending countless seminars on business, wealth building and real estate, we looked for ways to create passive income so we could then do what we wanted. We invested more than $100,000 in our education. Of course, by then I had lost touch with what I most wanted. We did get quite an education, however, which has paid for itself and more. Yet, in our hearts, something was still missing.

The last straw for me was when we got involved in foreclosure properties. Neither of us could have been more off track from our true wealth purpose. We learned a way to work this business with integrity, and those who have the right personality for dealing in foreclosure properties can do very well. Yet for us, we quickly discovered it wasn't about a simple transaction. We were not just buying houses. We were negotiating with people who were losing their homes and usually a lot more. It was devastating to hear their stories—illnesses, loss of jobs, divorce. Mostly these people were in great distress. It just broke my heart.

One day after receiving an angry phone call from a woman who was upset because we had obtained her phone number via her tenant, I had a bit of a meltdown. Mark and I had devised a little process to keep ourselves resolute on days when it felt difficult, which was daily for me. So I went to him and said, "I need five minutes to vent."

He said, "Okay," and got a timer. The idea was for me to release my pent-up frustration, then recommit and get back to work.

Well, for five minutes I let loose, saying things such as "I hate this business," and "I don't want to talk about foreclosures anymore," over and over again. Finally when I said, "I want to help people learn how to win in life," the timer went off.

Mark looked at me with a pleased expression on his face and said, "Hmmm, why don't you take another five minutes?"

I laughed behind my tears and said, "Sure." So off I went again, venting more of my frustration, mostly about how much I felt this direction was not right for me.

When I finished the second five minutes, I felt pretty tired, but I was relieved. I thanked Mark for listening, and I was ready to go back to work. Then he made an unexpected remark.

"Everything you said, I too have felt about this business. Maybe we need to rethink this." As we began to discuss it, I felt a dark cloud had lifted off of me. Suddenly, Mark said, "That's it. I quit."

I looked at him and said, "You quit?"

"That's right," he replied. "I quit."

Astonished, I said, "Okay, if you quit, I quit." Then we both fell on the floor laughing as we celebrated our graduation from that three-month stint in the foreclosure business.

Although, practically speaking, we were helping others by buying their homes before they lost them to a bank, in my heart I was never comfortable helping people in this way. We never bought a home in foreclosure, but we did help several people save their homes. Of course, that did not put money in our pockets, so we again found ourselves at a new crossroads.

I share this story to stir new questions that you may consider asking. Is there something—a job, an attitude or a pattern in your relationships—that you need to let go of? How do you go about making decisions for your life? Do you believe you have a purpose, and are you expressing this purpose on a daily basis? Do you love your life and the direction in which you are headed? Do you have a solid sense of self-respect? Have you made a daily practice of praying and asking for guidance? Do you really know your own core values, not just the values passed down to you? What moves you? What secret yearnings do you have? Are you in the right job, career or place in life? Is there something calling you right now? Have you sought the guidance of true experts who can help you get focused on *your* dreams, *your* goals and *your* unique way of creating wealth?

Until we examine the unexamined in our lives, and until we ask the hard questions of ourselves, we will likely flounder and struggle, and remain unfulfilled. The simplicity of asking for inner guidance was startling to me. I had prayed at different times in my life, usually when life wasn't going well and I wanted help from -- somewhere. The very idea of asking for guidance everyday and then following the response seemed, well, too easy. I will share here that for me, it was easy to pray and ask for help. The difficulty came in my fear of *receiving* guidance, because even when it was loud and clear, I was not always excited about what I heard.

As Mark has discussed earlier in the book, a common fear for many people is that they will receive guidance to do something they really don't want to do. I have to tell you honestly that your inner guardians *will* prod you to grow and move into the unknown. At first, this can seem intimidating, yet you will also reap the rewards of tremendous inner strength and power, self-confidence and peace of mind as your inner guidance moves you to find integrity with your soul. Many of us have become relaxed feeling as if we are in control and staying comfortable where we are. We may be withering on the vine, but at least we are *comfortable* and know what to expect.

After studying the subjects of wealth creation, life transition, finding your purpose in life, inner guidance and intuitive wisdom, I began to feel reassured by the experience of others who had ventured on this path before me. Each of them shared unique stories of how connecting with the wisdom of spirit will always lead toward our highest potential. The more conscious we become, the more empowered we are to move into the purpose of heart and soul. These stories all confirmed my own experience that the fear of silent knowledge will only get in our way.

I took a risk and decided to further my own experience. I started a daily practice of prayer to see what would happen. Well, it happened for me, too. I started receiving that powerful inner guidance, which Mark has shared so much about. It was calming how this felt so familiar and natural, even though I still found myself afraid. Two months into my new practice, I came to a certain point of choice. Would I remain stuck where I was in an unfulfilling life or would I surrender my ego-mind and trust that I was being led toward the fulfillment of my soul's desire and my true wealth purpose?

I began to exercise my prayer and "guidance muscle" daily. This has built a deeper trust in my ability to find clear direction through my connection to God and the infinite. There is enormous freedom and power in truth. It was not long before my new ways started to feel so ordinary that I wondered how I had functioned by hit-and-miss goal setting and planning.

Now, all of our plans and goals were surrendered as Mark and I flew by the seat of our faith. That's it really. When I let go of the way I thought everything worked, I made room for more interesting and surprising possibilities. My whole life has recalibrated. Wounds I carried from childhood finally healed. Areas where Mark and I were polarized began to transform. Resources and support were dropping into my life with little effort on my part. With near perfect timing, Mark and I came upon just the right experts who would help us know what to do next as we learned how to get out of our own way. Everything was changing as if by magic, simply because I was willing to ask for help. Even when I was scared out of my mind or displeased about the guidance, I did my best to follow it. My life is better, my attitudes have shifted, my relationships are deeper, I am more authentic and my creativity continues to blossom. This transformation took place in a short nine months.

At that time, I discovered my own tremendous gifts in supporting other people on their paths toward true wealth creation. I was able to facilitate transformation during their transitions and with their own discovery of their greatest gifts. As I delved into the depths of my own soul to find what I was being called to do, I heard simple instructions every day. I was encouraged to give kindness to others (and to myself). This alone would fulfill my purpose. I was guided to heal myself— spiritually, emotionally, mentally and physically—and to notice how my uplifted spirits served my purpose by raising my energy, opening my heart and prompting me to give compassion to others. I even became more patient when driving.

> Seek the guidance of true wealth experts who will help you get focused on *your* dreams, *your* goals, and *your* unique way of creating wealth from the inside out.

So don't get stuck thinking you have to find some huge, noble calling to be on track with fulfilling your purpose and having Wealth Inside Out. You may be guided, as I was, to simply heal yourself first. You may be guided to do something like raise the mood levels of your workplace by being kinder or more outspoken about changes you know would improve your surroundings. Perhaps you will heal your relationship with your mother or father. You may be suddenly compelled to do something even as simple as giving a compliment to someone you don't know. Maybe the business you have always dreamed of, but were too afraid to attempt until now, is what calls you. You could be guided to create enormous wealth by following your dreams and doing what you've always wanted to do.

Since opening my connection to intuitive wisdom, I have found that I can be in communication anytime about anything. Whatever you call your higher wisdom, God or the universe or simply the part of you that knows, this source is always by your side (and on your side), holding the best interests of your soul's development in the foreground. That is how you begin to create true wealth—wealth from the inside out.

Even when you resist or deny your innermost source, this life-giving support is always there.

My hope for each of you reading this book is that you open new possibilities for yourself that didn't seem possible before. I pray that you receive food for your heart and soul and that you take the first steps in transforming your life. May you have the strength and courage to follow your inner wisdom and fulfill your unique and precious true wealth purpose, so that when you depart this life, you can observe yourself with deep compassion and truly say, "I have no regrets."

The winds of grace are always blowing,
but it is you who must raise your sails.
Rabindranath Tagore, Indian poet and author (1861-1941)
Received the Nobel Prize in Literature in 1913

To Discover More about

Wealth Inside Out™ Trainings and

How They Will Help You Achieve

Your True Wealth Vision,

Please Visit Our Website

www.WealthInsideOut.com

Acknowledgments

Whenever I have looked at acknowledgments in other books, I've always wondered how there could be so many people involved. I mean, after all, it's only some written words and a print job, right?

Now that I have a clue, I hardly know where to begin thanking those who contributed to making this book happen. While many of the names mentioned throughout the book have been changed for various reasons, I want to acknowledge those who helped make this book possible. I'll begin by saying how grateful I am for the love of my life, Desirée, whose unwavering support has been ever-present, especially during the unsettling transitions we encountered on the road toward finding our purpose and creating Wealth Inside Out.

Next, I wish to thank editor Ann West for graciously taking on this project and sifting through the places where I no longer had clear perspective, providing direction and refinement to my writing. Thank you, Ann!

I also thank editor Tonja Grothe, who never having met me, nonetheless followed her instincts to step in and support this project. I'm still amazed at the synchronicity of our meeting and discovering the buffalo. Your steady encouragement is what at times kept me going during the writing phase. Thank you, Tonja!

I also thank Margot Edwards, who one night after our weekly yoga class blurted out her desire to help with this book. Your coaching on my writing skills was invaluable.

Thank you to those who took the time to preview various aspects of the book and give me your valuable feedback: Barry and Kipra Heermann, David and Annee Martin, Jim White, Mom and Dad Watson, Rainee Lehr, Greg Donovan, Bonnie Clawson, Doug Gelhaye, Greg and Dorothy Cole, Lori Wood, Doug and Tawney Barnard, Sheila Gale Kandlbinder, Jammi Barrington, Jerry Kaiser, Joyce Marvel-Benoist and Francois Benoist, Corinne Mayer, Bill Little, Fred Jealous, Carol Jordan, Margaret Merrill, Tracy and Sherry Watson, Donald Moine, Bob Korman, Amy Swan, Luke Aitken, Julie Rosenthal, Melanie Ziemniak, David Cates, Judith Arisman and Jerry Takigawa. Thank you to Mark Levine and all the folks at Bascom Hill Publishing Group for your expert help in putting the book together.

For the special times Desirée and I had with our wonderful R-Group—Barry, Kipra, Annee and David—all I can say is, what a wonderful ride together! Thank you so much for your support.

I wish to thank my teachers, coaches and expert mentors who helped us so much along the way. As I soaked up new skills and knowledge, your encouragement and support—ranging from a gentle embrace to a kick from behind—have made the difference in our success. Thank you.

To the many authors and teachers referenced in the book, I thank you for your wisdom and valuable insights, without which I would have been truly lost.

To my close friends and family who have been a foundational part of my life journey, I sincerely thank you for your ongoing love and support as I found my way. Even more, I thank you for having me in your life.

Please Note: Effort was made to provide accuracy when quoting others and to acknowledge original sources. If you find information to the contrary, please notify the publisher so we can make corrections in subsequent editions.

Bibliography

Aaron, Raymond. *The Monthly Mentor™: Discovering How to Do What You Love*. Richmond Hill, Ontario, Canada: Raymond Aaron Group, 2005.

Adrienne, Carol. *The Purpose of Your Life*. New York: William Morrow, 1998.

Andrews, Ted. *Animal Speak: The Spiritual and Magical Powers of Creatures Great and Small*. St. Paul, MN: Llewellyn, 2004.

Assaraf, John. *Cloning of Success: Home Mentoring Program*. San Diego, CA: The Street Kid, 2004.

Bethards, Betty. *The Dream Book: Symbols for Self-Understanding*. Boston, MA: Element, 1995.

Bohm, David. *Wholeness and the Implicate Order*. New York: Routledge, 2004.

Bridges, William. *The Way of Transition*. Cambridge, MA: Da Capo Press, 2001.

Childre, Doc, and Rozman, Deborah. *Transforming Stress: The Heartmath Solution for Relieving Worry, Fatigue and Tension*. Oakland, CA: New Harbinger, 2005.

Douglas, Mark, *Trading In The Zone*. Paramus, NJ: Prentice Hall, 2001.

Dyer, Wayne W. *The Power of Intention: Learning to Co-create Your World Your Way*. Carlsbad, CA: Hay House, 2004.

Hansen, Mark Victor, *Rich Results e-newsletter:* Newport Beach, CA: Mark Victor Hansen & Associates, 2005.

Heermann, Barry. *Noble Purpose: Igniting Extraordinary Passion for Life and Work*. Fairfax, VA: QSU Publishing Company, 2004.

Hill, Napoleon. *Think and Grow Rich. Meriden,* CT: The Ralston Society, 1938.

Jaworski, Joseph. *Synchronicity, The Inner Path of Leadership*. San Francisco: Berrett-Koehler, 1998.

Kiyosaki, Robert T., & Sharon Lechter L. *Rich Dad Poor Dad: What the Rich Teach Their Kids About Money that the Poor and Middle Class Don't*. Paradise Valley, AZ: TechPress, 1997.

Lefkoe, Morty. *Recreate Your Life: Transforming Yourself and Your World With the Decision Maker® process*. Fairfax, CA: DMI Publishing, 1997.

Lewis, James L. *The Dream Encyclopedia*. Canton, MI: Visible Ink Press, 1995.

Myss, Caroline, & Shealy, Norm. *The Science of Medical Intuition: Self-Diagnosis and Healing With Your Body's Energy Systems*. Boulder, CO: Sounds True, 2002.

Nani, Christel. *Diary of a Medical Intuitive: One Woman's Eye-Opening Journey From No-Nonsense E.R. Nurse to Open-Hearted Healer and Visionary*. Cayucos, CA: L.M. Press, 2004.

Newman, Paul, & Hotchner, A. E. *Shameless Exploitation in Pursuit of the Common Good*. New York: Random House, 2003.

Pond, David. *Chakras for Beginners: A Guide to Balancing Your Chakra Energies*. St. Paul, MN: Llewellyn, 2003.

Virtue, Doreen. *Divine Guidance*. New York: St. Martin's, 1998.

Wattles, Wallace D. *The Science of Getting Rich*. Wallace D. Wattles, 1910.

White, Jim. Circle of Success [Training Manual]. Monterey, CA: Jim White International, 2003.

To view photographs of the buffalo sightings, visit:
www.BuffaloTotem.com

To learn more about how Wealth Inside Out™ Trainings will help you learn how to become successful, please visit our Website at
www.WealthInsideOut.com

To download your supplementary
Wealth Creation Workbook, please go to
www.WealthCreationWorkbook.com

To obtain your Special Free Report
The 7 Biggest Mistakes Most Wealth Seekers Make and How You Can Avoid Them, please go to
www.SpecialWeatlhReport.com

About the Authors

Mark and Desirée Watson went from zero to become millionaires in less than three years using a powerful "inner technology" and a progression of skills that you can learn and use to achieve all of your most important goals. The processes they have developed work to rapidly improve virtually any area of your life or business, including your finances, relationships, self-confidence and peace of mind. Desirée and Mark's business backgrounds include book publishing, manufacturing, retail, construction, real estate investing and consulting. Mark and Desirée have dedicated more than 25 years to human achievement research and wealth creation dynamics. Whether it's financial, interpersonal, physical or spiritual wealth you desire, Mark and Desirée have the strategies you need to achieve mastery in all of those areas of your life. Mark and Desirée live on the Big Island of Hawaii and work with people all over the United States and Canada.

As cofounder of Wealth Inside Out™ Trainings, Mark Watson is dedicated to inspiring others to discover what holds true meaning in their lives. Mark started and very successfully operated companies in construction and in the greeting card industry. Mark and his wife, Desirée also owned a 72-unit apartment multiplex. Then through a catalytic life-changing event, he became clear about his true calling in the success-development field.

After more than 25 years of human potential research and study, Mark now reveals the secrets that contribute most strongly to having a totally successful life. Many people ask themselves the question Why do some people get what they want and others never seem to? In his work and in his writings, Mark fully answers this question and lays out a pathway that anyone who is interested in achieving a life of true success can follow.

Working with people all over the United States and Canada, Mark brings to you an unusually engaging mix of practical, down-to-earth strategies and leading-edge "inner technology" for creating true wealth and happiness in your life.

As cofounder of Wealth Inside Out™ Trainings, Desirée Watson loves helping others develop their own intuitive clarity and apply it in daily life. In addition to teaching and mentoring, she brings more than 25 years of inner development skills to the Wealth Inside Out™ trainings and coaching experience. Her business background includes book publishing, operations management, real estate investing, group facilitation and personal mentoring. Desirée has a naturally deep understanding and respect for the uniqueness of each individual and a gift for helping each person realize his or her true potential. Add this to her lifetime of practical experience and personal success, and you have a seasoned ally for enhancing your confidence and helping you achieve your most important goals in life.

Mark and Desirée Watson have developed powerful time-tested tools that empower you to live much more confidently. Their programs include Wealth Inside Out™ Mentoring, The Wealth Inside Out™ Seminar, Total Relationship Success® Coaching, The Pattern Busters® Skill Series and Executive Purpose® Trainings. You will learn more about these programs at www.WealthInsideOut.com

**Discover More Wealth Creation
Strategies at Our Website**

www.WealthInsideOut.com